'When the Bible speaks – G̲ ☑ **KT-431-763** ̲
World. Dr. Peckham's book enables us to understand not only
the character of Scripture, but also its contents and significance – it will be an enormously valuable aid to all who wish
to understand the significance of the Bible for today's world.'

Clive Calver,
President of the World Relief Corporation, America.

'Here is a racy and readable defence of the authority of the
Bible. Of especial value to young Christians, it sets out holy
Scripture as the Word of God, full and final in revelation and
authority.'

Dr. Herbert McGonigle,
Principal of the Nazarene Theological College,
Manchester, England.

'In a day when the authority of the Bible is rejected or under-
mined, even by many within the churches, it is gratifying to
find a preacher and teacher who has no such doubts.'

Dr. A. T. B. McGowan,
Director of the Highland Theological Institute.

'Here is a little booklet which deals with the subject of the
Bible in its quintessence, but in language which is simple, direct
and easily read. This little publication will appeal to young
and old alike and be read profitably by clergy and laity, with
equal profit. Its scope forbids that it be an exhaustive treatise
on this vital and wide-ranging topic, but all of the issues touched
upon are the inherently essential issues of which modern
Christians ought to be aware.

It gives me the greatest pleasure to recommend Dr. Colin
Peckham's publication to the general reading public and to
Christian believers in particular.'

Dr. Rex G. Mathie,
Former Principal of the Baptist Theological College,
Johannesburg

DR HERBERT McGONIGLE

The
Authority
of the
Bible

Colin N. Peckham

*To an honoured colleague
and esteemed friend
with warm Christian love*

Colin Peckham

Christian Focus

© Colin N. Peckham
ISBN 185792 436 3

Published in 1999
by
Christian Focus Publications
Geanies House, Fearn, Ross-shire
IV20 1TW, Great Britain

All Scripture references are taken
from the New King James Version.

Contents

PREFACE

This little book is at once apologetic, didactic and evangelistic. It stands in defence of historic Christianity's acceptance of the Bible as the only source of faith and practice; it gives instruction as to the contents, claims and authority of the Bible itself; and it brings home the saving and liberating message of these claims to the one who reads and trusts its truth.

If we were to neglect the Bible, regarding it as irrelevant or fictitious, and it is found to be true, our loss would be total, for we shall be called to give account before God on that great day.

It is therefore of supreme importance that we discover whether or not the Bible is divinely inspired and bears a message of eternal importance for us individually. This volume investigates this vital subject.

Colin N. Peckham

THE BIBLE

There is no other book like the Bible, no book that even remotely compares with the Bible. No other book has been so often printed or widely distributed in as many languages as the Bible. Its preservation is miraculous, its circulation amazing.

No other book has influenced human civilization, literature, art or government as has the Bible, nor has any book changed the lives of more people than the Bible. Its message is timeless. It will be as equally applicable to the twenty-first century as it was to the first. It fits men of all ages and is never out of date. It speaks with equal power to Jew or Gentile, black or white, old or young, learned or ignorant. Its authority is not that of a volume, but of a revelation. It is not an authorized collection of books, but a collection of authorized books.

It is human and divine. It has passed through the minds of men; it is written in the language of men; it is penned by the hands of men bearing their styles and characteristics. But it is supernatural, bringing thoughts which no human mind could ever have created. It concerns God who is Spirit, Light, Love and Holiness. It concerns man who is condemned because of his sin. No sinful man would have written so authoritatively as to condemn himself, and then take the utmost care to perpetuate the document and the condemnation. Yet it tells of infinite Love by which sinful man can be redeemed from his sin. The thoughts, the plan, the substance are far beyond the reaches of normal human thought patterns.

It is ancient and modern. It tells of the origin of the universe, the creation of the human race, the history of sin. It tells the story of a nomad called Abraham who lived 4,000 years ago. It tells of one of the greatest men ever to walk this earth, Moses, who lived 3,500 years ago. It gives the history of great empires and cities like Nineveh and Babylon, which are today but of archaeological interest.

Its last chapters were written almost 2,000 years ago, but it is so modern. It speaks to men and women, boys and girls today! It strikes the right chord and gives the clear call to the human heart today. It lays bare the thoughts and intentions of the soul, it exposes the evil within man. It is a living thing, a disturbing document, a probing instrument, a summoning missive, a healing balm, a comforting word. It meets the needs of men and women everywhere in this most modern of settings, the twenty-first century. How can such a book of antiquity be so relevant if not supernaturally inspired?

Surely we must investigate the Bible to discover its origins and ascertain whether the claim to it being the Word of God can be verified. If it is found to be but of human extraction, it can be treated on the same level as Homer, Virgil or Shakespeare. But if its pronouncements are divine, it has supreme authority and its substance and message must be taken seriously. Its warnings then have solemn and eternal implications and consequences, and its promises would result in lives being wonderfully transformed for ever.

How very important to determine the origin and authority of the Bible.

Chapter 1

ITS UNITY

The Bible is a unique phenomenon, wholly
unrivalled in the world of letters. It is a literary
marvel, a moral miracle.

It is not the product of one editor who chose his
contributors, mapped out his course of study, gave
each his assignment and then brought them all
together in a neatly bound volume. Its writing is as
diverse as can possibly be imagined. Here are sixty-
six different books, written by some forty authors
in three different languages and over a period of
about 1,600 years.

Hastings eloquently comments:

'The authorship of this Book is wonderful. Here are
words written by kings, by emperors, by princes, by
poets, by sages, by philosophers, by fishermen, by
statesmen, by men learned in the wisdom of Egypt,
educated in the schools of Babylon, trained up at the
feet of the Rabbis in Jerusalem. It was written by
men in exile, in the desert, in shepherds' tents, in
"green pastures" and "beside still waters". Among
its authors we find the tax-gatherer, the herdsman,
the gatherer of sycamore fruit; we find poor men,
rich men, statesmen, preachers, exiles, captains,
legislators, judges; men of every grade and class are
represented in this wonderful volume, which is in
reality a library, filled with history, genealogy,

ethnology, law, ethics, prophecy, poetry, eloquence, medicine, sanitary science, political economy and perfect rules for the conduct of personal and social life. It contains all kinds of writing; but what a jumble it would be if sixty-six books were written in this way by ordinary men.'

The vast differences in every aspect of its production are obvious to even the most casual observer. The authors are so different and remote from one another that they would not have been acquainted nor could they have conspired together for either evil or good purposes. They had enormous differences in cultural backgrounds, writing in Egypt, Babylon, Israel, Asia Minor and Europe. Their understanding of events and circumstances, of values and concepts, of religions and philosophies must have been influenced by the milieu in which they lived.

They spoke of hygiene, of science, of history, both of the contemporary world and of Israel's part in it. Their writings were moral and theological, practical and down to earth, forensic and legislative, national and personal, prophetic and apocalyptic, advisory and authoritative. They uttered both anathema and benediction. There is law and history, poetry and prose, wisdom and ethic.

The styles of writing vary with every author, and at times within his own writings. There is that of the flowing orator, the wise counsellor, the fiery prophet, the explicit denunciator, the tender lover, the meticulous investigator, the accurate historian,

14

the logical theologian, the dreaming visionary.

What a dreadful muddle it would all be if there was no central controlling influence; but it all fits together like a hand in a glove. The unity is miraculous and marvellous.

1. The Nature of the Unity
R. A. Torrey states:

> 'It is not a superficial unity, but a profound unity. On the surface we often find apparent discrepancy and disagreement, but, as we study, the apparent discrepancy and disagreement disappear, and the deep underlying unity appears. The more deeply we study, the more complete do we find the unity to be.'[1]

The Unity is Structural
The Pentateuch is the basis of all Old Testament teaching and prophecy. The Gospels, which tell of the life of Christ, are also the basis of all New Testament teaching. In the Old Testament we have history from Joshua to Esther, and in the New Testament we have history in the book of Acts. Teaching and devotion is given in the Old Testament from Job to the Song of Solomon, and in the New Testament in the Epistles. Prophecy in the Old Testament is from Isaiah to Malachi and in the New in Revelation. The pattern is set in the Old Testament and followed in the New Testament. There is a marvellous unity without any planning in its composition or substance. Each wrote as they were moved by the Spirit and the consequent full-

orbed and structured teaching was the result. Rene Pache observed that we have:

In the Old Testament	salvation prepared
In the Gospels	salvation effected
In the Acts	salvation propagated
In the Epistles	salvation explained
In Revelation	salvation fulfilled.[2]

That which the Old Testament promises, the New Testament presents. What is the longing in the Old Testament is the satisfaction in the New. 'Oh, that I knew where I might find Him!' becomes 'We have found Him' (Job 23:3; John 1:45). Graham Scroggie states:

In the Old Testament Christ is predicted; in the Gospels He is present; in Acts He is proclaimed; in the Epistles He is possessed; and in Revelation he is predominant. Christ is the focus of all history, prophecy and type. Divine revelation converges on Him in the Old Testament, and emerges from Him in the New Testament. Both parts of the Revelation meet in Him; the one as preparation, and the other as realization.... God and man meet in the One who is the God-Man.[3]

The Gospels in the New Testament are not merely repetitions, but they present various aspects of the life of Christ. Four complementary portraits of Christ are seen.

The styles of the writers are so different. Matthew is methodical and massive; Mark is conversational, graphic, concise, abrupt, vigorous and forceful; Luke is careful, artistic and graceful; John is abstract and profound.

In Matthew Christ has come to fulfil (5:17);
In Mark Christ has come to minister (10:45);
In Luke Christ has come to save (19:10);
In John Christ has come to reveal (5:43).

Matthew presents Christ the King;
Mark presents Christ the Servant;
Luke presents Christ the Son of Man;
John presents Christ the Son of God.

The description of the four living creatures in Ezekiel 1:10, 10:14, Rev. 4:7, represent the different aspects of Christ's character as portrayed in the gospels. They had the faces of:

A Lion:	Christ the King in Matthew;
An Ox:	Christ the Servant in Mark;
A Man:	Christ the Son of Man in Luke;
An Eagle:	Christ the Son of God in John.

The Book of Acts is the historical outworking of that life through the apostles and disciples.

Concerning the Epistles, Bancroft writes: 'There are five epistle writers; Paul, especially the epistle of Faith; Peter, of Hope; John, of Love; James, of Good Works; and Jude, of Warning against Apostasy. Thus without human design or intentional co-operation, all the necessary ground is covered without overlapping.'[4]

The Unity is Composite

In the Old Testament there is anticipation; in the New Testament there is realization. The Old witnesses to the New and the New confirms the Old. The New is the outgrowth of the Old. In the Old there are the shadows and types, and in the New, those shadows become realities. If therefore the Old Testament is the Word of God, the New must be also, or, if the New is the Word of God, so too then must be the Old. They stand or fall together, for they speak with one voice and bear the same message. It has been said:

The New is in the Old contained
The Old is in the New explained
The New is in the Old enfolded
The Old is in the New unfolded
The New is in the Old concealed
The Old is in the New revealed.

The Unity is Didactic

While there are various interpretations of the meaning of different Scriptures, there is perfect harmony across the whole of the Scripture record. The teaching is not contradictory. Parts of the Scripture are not in opposition to other parts. Some parts are allegorical and some are factual, some are mystical and some are plain, some are theological and some are historical, but all dovetail together and form a unified message of God, man, sin and salvation.

The Unity is Historical

While the Bible begins with the origins and history of the human race, it soon focuses on the chosen family of Abraham. This resulted in the record of the nation which sprang from him – Israel. The history of the people of God is narrated. In the New Testament, the story continues, only the people of God are now the children of Abraham by faith in Abraham's Seed – Jesus of Nazareth, God's Son and our Saviour. It is salvation history from the pictures of Christ in creation in Genesis, to the consummation of it all when He leads those whom He has redeemed by His blood into their heavenly home in the book of Revelation.

The Unity is Prophetic

This is an inexplicable miracle, and prophecy is one of the greatest proofs of the divine origin and authority of the Bible. Many of the Old Testament prophecies are fulfilled in the New Testament and the New Testament itself is full of prophecies, all of which are in harmony with the forward-looking Old Testament prophecies. The specific prophetic chapters in the Synoptic Gospels, Matthew 24, Mark 13 and Luke 21, accord with the prophecies of Daniel and those of John in the Apocalypse. One great plan is unfolded, a plan which is absolute proof of the Divine origin of the Scriptures.

The Unity is Spiritual

The Bible is pervaded by one vitalizing spirit, the Spirit of God. One Spirit flows through it all,

19

inspiring and directing. If the Spirit of God was not behind all these diverse writers, how would it be possible for this unity to prevail? There are many writers but one Author. There is no contradiction, no confusion of types, and no collision of doctrine. There is a spiritual perspective, outlook and attitude which runs through everything. We are drawn to God by the Spirit of God and the means of grace which have remained the same for thousands of years. Pictures, types and shadows find their spiritual reality in Christ. The Book is alive and it speaks to our hearts by the Spirit of God. Whether we read in Genesis, or Ezra, or Zechariah, or Mark, or Romans, or Peter, it speaks to us. It is like no other book. It lives because God is the Author, and He lives today just as He lived in the days of Abraham. His voice is as strong today as it was then. We hear it; we know it; it is the communication of Spirit to spirit. The Book speaks with one message. It speaks to the heart. Its unity is spiritual.

2. The Growth of the Unity

The unity is not only broad and extensive, deep and pervasive, it is developing and expansive. It is a unity that grows, and it has value throughout its growth as well as in the end product.

It is the relationship of seed to plant, of plant to blossom, of blossom to harvest. The germ thought is planted in Genesis, develops in the Old Testament, finds fulfilment in the New, and on occasions, looks forward to a still further fulfilment in the coming Kingdom.

In Genesis 3:15, we have the great prophecy in the Garden of Eden, 'And I will put enmity between you and the woman, and between your seed and her Seed; He shall bruise your head, and you shall bruise His heel.' Down the years there was conflict between the people of God and the forces of evil. This culminated in the mighty clash at Calvary when the poisonous serpent bit the heel of the Seed of the woman filling Him with its evil poison, ('He made Him who knew no sin to be sin for us' [2 Cor. 5:21]), and causing His death. Yet He rose to bruise the head of the Serpent and strip him of his power. Jesus is the mighty conqueror over sin and death, and over Satan and hell. There will, however, be a future time when Satan will receive the final sentence and be put away for ever (Rev. 20:10). The prophecy was given in Genesis, it was partially fulfilled in Old Testament days, it found reverberating fulfilment in Christ's death on Calvary, and will be conclusively fulfilled in Satan's final judgment. The Scripture has been shown to be one in prophecy, type, anti-type and in its final fulfilment. The seed has germinated, the plant has flourished, the bud has blossomed and the harvest will finally be gathered.

Abel offered a sacrifice, and, much later, so did Abraham. During the time of Moses some 500 years later, the Levitical system of sacrifices was introduced. That which began early in Genesis had developed into an ordered, established, national institution, which eventually found fulfilment in the

21

death of Jesus Christ. The concept began, grew, pointed forward and saw a satisfactory completion in the offering of the Lamb of God. In the book of Revelation, we see the completion of the story:

> 'For You were slain, and have redeemed us to God by Your blood...' (Rev. 5:9)

> 'These are the ones who come out of the great tribulation, and washed their robes and made them white in the blood of the Lamb' (Rev. 7:14)

> 'And they sing the song of Moses, the servant of God, and the song of the Lamb...' (Rev. 15: 3).

Redemption is complete with the worshipful song of the redeemed in heaven. That which began in Genesis comes to a conclusion in Revelation.

Various themes could be taken to illustrate the growth of the unity through the Bible.

3. The Extent of the Unity

1. Revelation

Spiritual values enshrined in the Old Testament had a life which extended into the New Testament. The Bible is the history of revelation. God revealed Himself through imperfect man with false presuppositions, imperfect outlook and limited spiritual capacity. He was therefore limited in His revelation by the medium which He chose. The Bible story is the unfolding of divine revelation through men. God laid hold of men who acted under

His direction and mediated His thoughts and principles to men. If this is true, then there should be a unity throughout all the divine writings, even though there will be a diversity because of the different abilities and capacities of the men who received the revelation.

This unity is a unity of process and development requiring eventually the full revelation which God gave in Christ Jesus. A continuing thread runs through events which may seem at first to be different and unrelated but are found to be interwoven in the process of biblical revelation. To regard the New Testament with veneration and to acknowledge Christ as God's revelation to man, and yet ignore the Old Testament is impossible, for the Old Testament is the background to the New Testament, and the New is the fulfilment and outworking of the Old.

Old Testament typology prefigures Christ and the Church. It anticipates the Cross and prepares for it. The creative religious ideas and the ethical impulse given through Moses were carried forward into the New Testament.

In the Old Testament we have a Monotheism with an ethical religion which sprang from the character of God and His demands. The revelation of God is dynamic. If Yahweh, or Jehovah, is the only true God, and it is His desire to reveal Himself to man then all must hear and all must worship Him alone. The religion of Yahweh must then move from its narrow beginnings to the broad masses of the world. The revelation of God is missionary and finds expression not merely in the few proselytes to the Jewish religion, but in the extensive activities and missionary advance of the church age.

Israel's unique honour was not only to receive but to communicate revelation and to perfect the calling, 'I will give You as a covenant to the people, as a light to the Gentiles' (Is. 42:6). This prophecy finds fulfilment in Christ and in the new Israel of God, the church, as it spreads the revelation of God to the ends of the earth. It has translated the Jewish Bible into thousands of languages and sent it all over the world, together with the New Testament which flows from it. The mission committed to Israel has been accepted and carried out by the Church.

The continuing thread of revelation makes this library a book, and makes the anticipated Messiah the Saviour of the world. The amazing expression of the unity of biblical revelation is a strong evidence of its divine origin.

2. Religion

It is claimed that there is a vast difference between the role and methods, and the substance and message of the priests and the prophets.

The prophets denounced the sacrificial system. Amos says: 'I despise your feast days ... your burnt offerings ... I will not accept them' (Amos 5:21, 22). Hosea exclaims: 'I desire mercy and not sacrifice' (Hos. 6:6). Isaiah says: 'to what purpose is the multitude of your sacrifices?' (Is. 1:11 ff). It is deduced therefore that we have two separate concepts of the revealed religion, priestly as opposed to prophetic.

It would seem, however, that modern doubts are being read back into the texts, for there are many passages in the Old Testament which speak of the priests and prophets standing together. The difference lay in the realm of the spirit rather than the function. The prophets called for obedience, without which the sacrifices were merely a show of meaningless religion. The prophets did not deny the need for sacrifices but showed that the sacrifices were invalidated because of the lack of obedience and righteousness. Jeremiah announced the destruction of the temple, not because he opposed the sacrificial system, but because they had polluted it and were trusting in the form of religion without following the God who had given them the temple in order that they might approach Him in sincerity and follow Him in obedience. Obedience and righteousness were the important issues.

Sacrifice as an external act, unrelated to the spirit, had no value. The attitude of heart was all important, and pardon would be granted to the repentant worshipper. The prophets could see no repentance, no cry for forgiveness, no plea for fellowship; the heart of the people was far from God. The hollow and meaningless sacrifices therefore, were denounced, but this did not mean that the prophets denounced all sacrifices. The sacrificial system had been given for men to approach God. If, however, it were regarded as a mere formality, it would be worthless.

H. H. Rowley says: 'The Old Testament nowhere teaches that sacrifice is valid without relation to the spirit.'[5]

The Law and the Prophets both claim that sacrifice and ritual acts were meaningless without the spirit of the worshipper. Attitude of heart and dedication of life accompany the sacrificial system. There is thus not a divergence of teaching, but a significant bond running through all the diversity of the Old Testament forming a unity in relation to the ministry of both priest and prophet.

Critics who have attempted to discredit the Bible by setting at variance the two main ministries in the Old Testament have signally failed, for on closer examination, both priest and prophet are seen to speak with one voice in drawing men and women, by sacrifice and obedience, to a God of righteousness and holiness.

3. Biblical Concepts
Monotheism characterizes the Bible. The only permissible worship was that of one God as is evidenced in the Ten Commandments. Jewish theology is almost built on Deuteronomy 6:4, 'Hear, O Israel: The LORD our God, the LORD is one.' God is not to be represented by idols. That idols were made at times does not disprove the fact of the divine displeasure at their existence. Christ is not a

26

threat to monotheism for His deity is evident in the New Testament, and the seeds of His deity are seen in the Old Testament.

God's Compassion is perceived in several places. When the Israelites were suffering in Egypt, He said, 'I have surely seen the oppression of My people ... have heard their cry ... I know their sorrows. So I have come down to deliver them' (Ex. 3:7, 8). Then followed the mighty Exodus. 'The LORD, the LORD God, merciful and gracious' (Ex. 34:6).

Israel, by her sin, often over the many years merited the punishment of God, yet in His compassion He sent her prophets who called her to repentance and restored her to divine favour.

God's great act of compassion, of course, is expressed in the life and death of Jesus. By this death, His compassion for a lost world is clearly seen.

God's Faithfulness. He is dependable and constant, not arbitrary and changeable. Heathen gods were fickle, of dubious morals and of doubtful character, but all the Old Testament characters found God to be always the same. In the New Testament we read that with God there 'is no variation or shadow of turning' (James 1:17). The faithfulness and unchangeable nature of God is evident throughout Scripture, and His character remains unblemished by moral aberrations.

God's Holiness. His moral character shines forth throughout both Old and New Testaments. In fact, the holiness of God is one of the chief distinguishing marks of the Old Testament. Having the root meanings of 'separation', 'radiance and brightness', and 'free from defect', the word 'holy' was applied to God, 'the Holy One of Israel'. The word 'holy' (qodesh) 'comes in the first place among the Hebrews to refer to Jehovah alone ... Holiness is of God and not of man' says Snaith.[6] This concept is maintained all through the Old Testament. There is no contradiction. No prophet declared that Baal, or Moloch, or Ashteroth was holy. Centuries went by, but uncannily, although there must have been massive pressures for change, the character of God retained its moral distinctiveness. God was morally impeccable; He was holy.

God's Righteousness. God is righteous in His hatred of oppression as seen in the Exodus story. Amos makes charges of social injustice. Hosea is more general but roundly condemns their worship while they continue in their sin. Micah and Isaiah likewise condemn rebellion and evil. Snaith declares, 'Jehovah, say these prophets, one and all, demands right conduct from His worshippers ... Their standard was what they themselves knew of the very nature of God Himself.'[7]

Themes such as the other attributes of God, as well as His initiative, His covenant relationship with Israel and many more can be traced through the

Old Testament and into the New Testament. Amazingly there is a unity of thought, a unity which stretches over more than 1500 years. Why are there no contradictions? Why is there no dissent? Why do the prophets not vie with one another to show different aspects of what they feel God would be like – aspects which, in the atmosphere of heathen worship, should be different from other biblical writings?

Astoundingly, they speak with one voice over such a long period of time. Some people have tried to show contradictions in Scripture – a few trivial discrepancies – which, if the Scriptures are correctly understood, may be satisfactorily explained. But how does one explain this? The phenomenal unity of teaching, of spiritual understanding, is an overwhelming argument for the uniqueness and divinity of the whole of the Word of God. How else can it be explained if not by the fact that the writers were being guided by one Spirit, one Author, one eternal God?

The unity of the Scriptures can now be seen to be a very strong proof that the Bible is divinely inspired.

Chapter 2

ITS INHERENT AUTHORITY

A great proportion of Scripture is definitely stated to consist of the Word of God. The phrase 'Thus saith the Lord,' and similar phrases 'are found 3808 times in the Old Testament.'[1] In fact, 'God said', 'the Lord said', 'God spoke' and similar statements occur 'over 700 times in the Pentateuch. In the historical books there is a similar list of considerably over 400 ... some 150 times in Isaiah alone.... almost 350 times in Ezekiel.'[2] Of these figures, W. E. Vine states, 'cumulatively it stamps the whole book with a divine impress.'[3] Leander Munhall points out that no fewer than twenty times does the prophet Isaiah explicitly declare that his writings are the 'words of the Lord.'[4] Almost 100 times Jeremiah says, 'The word of the Lord came unto me' or declares that he was writing 'the words of the Lord.' To Ezekiel it is said, 'Son of man, receive into your heart all My words that I speak to you, and hear with your ears. And go, get to the captives, to the children of your people, and speak to them and tell them, "Thus says the LORD God"' (Ezek. 3:10, 11).

Daniel said, 'Yet I heard the sound of His words' (Dan. 10: 9).

Hosea said, 'The word of the LORD that came to Hosea' (Hos. 1:1).

We read, 'The word of the LORD that came to Joel' (Joel 1:1).

Amos said, 'Hear this word that the LORD has spoken' (Amos 3:1).

Obadiah said, 'Thus says the LORD God' (Obad. 1:1).

We read, 'The word of the LORD came to Jonah' (Jonah 1:1). And again,

'The word of the LORD that came to Micah' (Mic. 1:1).

Nahum said, 'Thus says the LORD' (Nah. 1:12).

Habakkuk wrote, 'The LORD answered me, and said' (Hab. 2:2).

We read, 'The word of the LORD which came to Zephaniah' (Zeph. 1:1). And,

'The word of the LORD came by Haggai the prophet' (Hag. 1:1). And again,

'The word of the LORD came to Zechariah' (Zech. 1:1).

'The word of the LORD to Israel by Malachi' (Mal. 1:1).

In this last of the Old Testament books, twenty-four times we read, 'Thus saith the Lord.'

The Scriptures are called 'oracles of God' (Rom. 3:2), 'the word of God' (Luke 8:11), 'the word of the Lord' (Acts 13:48), 'the word of life' (Phil. 2:16), 'the word of Christ' (Col. 3:16), 'the word of truth' (Eph. 1:13) and 'the word of faith' (Rom. 10:8). The Bible never in a single instance says the thoughts of the writers were inspired, but that they received inspired words from God.

The way in which the writers speak of the Scriptures as the work of the Spirit of God indicates clearly that they thought that the words which they received from God were inspired. David says, for instance, 'The Spirit of the LORD spoke by me, and His Word was on my tongue' (2 Sam. 23:2).

The psalmist speaks of the moral quality of the Scriptures in Psalm 12:6: 'The words of the LORD are pure words ... purified seven times.' 'The law of the LORD is perfect, converting the soul; the testimony of the LORD is sure, making wise the simple. The statutes of the LORD are right, rejoicing the heart: the commandment of the LORD is pure, enlightening the eyes' (Ps. 19:7, 8). In Proverbs 30:5 we read, 'Every word of God is pure.'

Zacharias, the father of John the Baptist, 'was filled with the Holy Spirit, and prophesied, saying ... He (God) spoke by the mouth of His holy prophets' (Luke 1: 67, 70), attributing the words of the prophets to God.

In the ten verses of Mary's magnificat (Luke 1:46-55), there are numerous references and allusions to Old Testament Scriptures. She quotes 13 times from the Psalms (33, 34, 71, 83, 86, 98, 99, 103, 111, 118, 132, 138), 3 times from Samuel (1 Sam. 2 – twice, and 1 Sam. 1:11), and once from each of the following: Genesis 17:19, Exodus 2:6, Ezekiel 21:26, Job 22:9. There are about 20 references from 18 chapters in the Old Testament. Her whole thought pattern is biblical as she links one Scripture to another. She welcomes the news of the coming Messiah and magnifies the Lord by joyfully reciting many Scriptural words and phrases. For her these held eternal value for she closed her great song with the words, 'As He (God) spoke to our fathers, to Abraham, and to his seed forever.' She stamped the verses which she had quoted from the Old Testament with divine authority.

The New Testament Writers' View of the Old Testament

The Tenach, i.e. the Jewish Bible or our Old Testament, was Christ's Bible, and His attitude towards it was theirs. A rejection of the apostles' teaching therefore is a rejection of the teaching of Christ. 'The apostles appealed directly to the letter of the Old Testament to authorize their teaching and consistently presented the Christian faith as the fulfilment of the Scriptures,' says Bruce Milne.[5]

These men had been specifically chosen by Christ to be His disciples (Luke 5:27, 6:12-16, John 17:6). He gave them a special endowment of the Spirit (John 20:22, cf.. Acts 1:5, 8), promising the Holy Spirit to guide them in their teaching and witnessing (John 14:26, 15:26, 16:13). He commissioned them to go and teach 'all things that I have commanded you' (Matt. 28:20). On His auth-ority they went, claiming direct insight and referring to the Old Testament as their basic message.

Mark tells how the Lord quotes from Psalm 110 declaring that the words were uttered by David 'by the Holy Spirit' (Mark 12:36).

John says, 'I have written to you, young men,

because you are strong, and the word of God abides in you' (1 John 2:14). Because John wrote this epistle so late he could actually have meant the New Testament, but the Old Testament Scriptures are nevertheless in view as 'the word of God.'

What can be said of the book of the Revelation which, just because it is revelation, is the Word of God? Professor Milligan wrote of this book, 'It is a perfect mosaic of passages from the Old Testament, at one time quoted verbally, at another referred to by distinct allusion, now taken from one scene in Jewish history and now again from two or three together.'[6] Scroggie states that, 'out of the total number of 404 verses in this book, about 265 verses contain Old Testament language, and about 550 references are made to Old Testament passages.' He deduces from these facts: 'If this book is a revelation from and of God, seeing that the book is substantially the Old Testament in a new combination, therefore the Old Testament must be a revelation from and of God.'[7]

The writer to the Hebrews quotes many times from the Old Testament, nearly always omitting the name of the writer quoted, and attributing the quoted Scriptures to the Holy Spirit, or saying simply, 'He said.' The writer says, right at the beginning 'God ... spoke in time past to the fathers by the prophets' (Heb. 1:1). He says in chapter 3:7 'therefore, as the Holy Spirit says ...' and then quotes Psalm 95:8, 'Do not harden your hearts, as in the rebellion.' He does the same with Jeremiah 31:33, 34, 'This is the covenant ... I will put My law in their minds, and write it on their hearts ...' for he quotes this passage prefacing it with the words, 'the Holy Spirit had said before ...' (Heb. 10:15).

The whole book of the Hebrews is based upon the Old Testament and he interprets it in relation to Jesus Christ and New Testament revelation. If the Old Testament is not the Word of God, the foundation to this whole epistle is swept away.

James speaks of looking 'into the perfect law of liberty' (James 1:25), which of course is the Old Testament Scriptures. The whole epistle of James is based on the Old Testament; its language and atmosphere are those of the Old Testament.

There are only twenty-five verses in Jude but a number of Old Testament characters and historical events are mentioned. He speaks of the land of Egypt, Sodom and Gomorrah, Moses, Cain, Balaam, Enoch, Adam. Jude rests wholly on the Old Testament for substance and spiritual teaching.

These writers take for granted that the Old Testament is accurate. In its history, God is revealed and speaks with eternal authority.

Peter claims that in Psalm 41, the Holy Spirit spoke by the mouth of David (Acts 1:16).

Peter prayed, 'God ... who by the mouth of Your servant David have said: Why did the nations rage, and the people plot vain things?' (Acts 4:25 quoting Ps. 2:1). Peter states categorically that God spoke through David's lips. He also states, 'The God of glory appeared to our father Abraham ... and said to him' (Acts 7:2, 3). Peter certainly believed that the Old Testament was a divine revelation and that God spoke to and through the fathers and the prophets.

Speaking of this present salvation, Peter says, 'of this salvation the prophets have inquired and searched diligently, who prophesied of the grace that would come to you, searching what, or what manner of time, the Spirit of Christ who was in them was indicating when He testified beforehand the sufferings of Christ and the glories that would follow' (1 Pet. 1:10, 11). What the prophets wrote therefore, – for that is what he means – was communicated to them by the Spirit. Interestingly it is the 'Spirit of *Christ*,' who was yet to come, who was in them, indicating the oneness of the Trinity, for in many places in the Old Testament we read of the Spirit of God speaking in and through the prophets. Here Peter calls the Spirit of God in the Old Testament, the 'Spirit of Christ'. This divine Spirit was in the prophets, and He testified and prophesied concerning Christ. The written prophecy which is in view here is thus divinely inspired.

Another strong statement from Peter is in 2 Peter 1:21: 'prophecy never came by the will of man, but holy men of God spoke as they were moved by the Holy Spirit.' The participle 'moved' may be translated 'when moved', so we have here the knowledge that holy men wrote when moved upon by the Spirit to do so.

The participle is also passive and this means 'to

37

be moved on or upon'. Men, therefore, did not write when or what they pleased, but when prompted and urged to do so by the constraint of the Holy Spirit who would reveal truths to them and guide them in their record of such truths. Holy men of God wrote in obedience to God's command that which God revealed to them. If that is so, then they wrote without error, and the Bible is the very Word of God.

Professor Orr states:

'Taking the extensive prophetic literature of the Old Testament, it will not be denied that this claims to be produced under direct divine inspiration. The prophets ..., called and equipped for their special work by God, receiving their message from His hand, delivering them under the solemn sanction of a "Thus saith the Lord," accrediting them with supernatural prediction, speak and write with an authority which cannot be taken from them. Their writings, accordingly, answer in the highest degree to the test of inspiration.'[9]

To Paul the Old Testament was the unfolding of the divine purpose and providence. He speaks of 'the gospel of God, which He promised before through His prophets in the Holy Scriptures' (Rom. 1:1, 2).

He personifies the Word implying its inviolable authority: 'What does the Scripture say?' (Rom. 4:3); 'Do you not know what the Scripture says of Elijah?' (Rom. 11:2); 'Nevertheless what does the Scripture say? Cast out the bondwoman and her son'

38

(Gal. 4:30); 'For the Scripture says to Pharaoh ...' (Rom. 9:17); 'For the Scripture says, Whoever believes on Him will not be put to shame' (Rom. 10:11); 'But the Scripture has confined all under sin' (Gal. 3:22); 'And the Scripture, foreseeing that God would justify the nations by faith ...' (Gal. 3:8). The Scripture looked ahead and saw what would happen. Paul sees the Scriptures as the body of divine revelation – as the very voice and words of God. The Scriptures not only speak with one voice, they see as well. They have vision.

Scroggie claims that Paul actually

'quotes from twenty-five of its thirty-nine books. According to Westcott and Hort, there are seventy-four quotations in Romans, twenty-nine in 1 Corinthians, twenty in 2 Corinthians, thirteen in Galatians, twenty-one in Ephesians, six in Philippians, four in Colossians, seven in 1 Thessalonians, nine in 2 Thessalonians, two in 1 Timothy, four in 2 Timothy and three in Titus. These Scriptures are appealed to as being authoritative, as setting forth the mind and acts of God.'[10]

Paul said that he worshipped God, 'believing all things which are written in the Law and in the prophets' (Acts 24:14). His acceptance of the Old Testament was total and final. To Timothy he says, 'that from childhood you have known the Holy Scriptures, which are able to make you wise for salvation through faith which is in Christ Jesus' (2 Tim. 3:15). Not only are they authoritative but they

39

are powerful and are life-transforming.

In 1 Timothy 5:18, we have a particularly significant statement: 'For the Scripture says, You shall not muzzle an ox while it treads out the grain.' And, 'the labourer is worthy of his wages.' The first quotation is from Deuteronomy 25:4, and the second from Luke 10:7. The quotations from both Old and New Testament are called 'Scripture'. They are equally invested with divine authority and equally express the mind of God.

Paul commands that his letter to the Colossians be 'read in the church' (Col. 4:16). The Old Testament was read in the congregation, and now Paul's letter is to be read alongside these accepted and acknowledged Scriptures, placing it in the same class.

There has been conflict over 2 Timothy 3:16 where Paul declares that all Scripture is inspired by God. The word 'inspired' means literally 'God-breathed'. It is composed of two Greek words, 'theos' – God, and 'pnein' – to breathe. The term, 'given by inspiration', signifies that the words of the Old Testament of which Paul is speaking, are the result of God's influence upon the writers.

The 'pnein' is described in Liddel & Scott's lexicon as 'to blow, breathe, to exhale, to breathe hard, pant, gasp' etc. It is a term that denotes a forcible respiration, and conscious breathing.

'Inspiration, then, as defined by Paul in this passage, is the strong, conscious inbreathing of God into men, and the Old Testament is therefore just

40

as much the Word of God as though God spoke every single word of it with His own lips,' says William Evans.[11]

The Authorised Version reads 'All Scripture is given by inspiration of God, and is profitable for doctrine, for reproof, for correction, for instruction in righteousness.' The Revised Version reads, 'Every Scripture inspired of God is also profitable for teaching, for reproof, for correction, for instruction which is in righteousness.' Some have said that there is no essential difference, and that it would be absurd to think that Paul meant to speak of a line which no one could see running up and down the Bible, so that some of it was inspired and some not.

Others, and they are in the vast majority, declare that this RV is erroneous, noting that if Paul had said that 'All Scripture that is divinely inspired is also profitable', he would virtually have said that there is some Scripture that is not divinely inspired. Human rationalism would have a field day, each man rejecting whatever passage, which to him was not inspired nor profitable, and each one differing in his interpretation. The result of that would be that there would be no Bible left. The RV rendering is false because the revisers refused to render the same Greek construction elsewhere in the same way, convicting them of error.

In Hebrews 4:13 for instance, we read: 'All things are naked and opened unto the eyes of Him with whom we have to do' (AV). The form and construction of this verse is identical to that of 2 Timothy 3:16, but if we were to translate this as the revisers have 2 Timothy 3:16, it would read: 'All naked things are also open to the eyes of Him with whom we have to do.' All naked things are also open things! There is no 'also' here nor in 2 Timothy 3:16.

In 1 Timothy 4:4 also, we read: 'For every creature of God is good and nothing to be refused.' (AV) The revisers' principles would render this, 'every good creature of God is also nothing to be rejected.' The place of the word 'is', which must be supplied in translation, is directly before the word 'inspired' and not after it.

The great rationalistic scholar De Wette, confessed candidly that the rendering that the revisers had adopted cannot be defended. In his German version of the text he gave the sense thus: 'Every sacred writing, i.e. of the canonical Scriptures, is inspired of God and is useful for doctrine, etc.' Bishops Moberly and Wordsworth, Archbishop Trench, and others of the Revision committee disclaimed any responsibility for the rendering. Dean Burgon pronounced it 'the most astonishing as well as calamitous blunder of the age.' It was condemned by Dr. Tregelles, the only man ever pensioned by the British government for scholarship.

In accordance with the weight of testimony, therefore, we hold to the rendering of the Authorized Version, and claim that 'all Scripture is equally and fully inspired of God.'[12]

The apostles and New Testament writers most certainly believed that the Old Testament was the Word of God.

The New Testament Writers' View of the New Testament

In 1 Corinthians 2:9 and 10, Paul refers to Isaiah 64:4 when he says, 'But as it is written: Eye has not seen, nor ear heard, nor have entered into the heart of man, the things which God has prepared for those who love Him. But God has revealed them to us through His Spirit.' Paul actually attributes the content and communication of the message to be of God.

In 1 Corinthians 2:12, 13, we read, 'Now we have received, not the spirit of the world, but the Spirit who is from God, that we might know the things that have been freely given to us by God. These things we also speak, not in words which man's wisdom teaches but which the Holy Spirit teaches, comparing spiritual things with spiritual.' This bold assertion can only be made because of his complete confidence in the commission and authority of Christ, and because of his conscious knowledge of the Spirit's indwelling, teaching and direction.

In 1 Corinthians 14:37, Paul says, 'If anyone thinks himself to be a prophet or spiritual, let him acknowledge that the things which I write to you are the commandments of the Lord.'

In 1 Thessalonians 2:13, we find another strong

claim, 'When you received the word of God which you heard from us, you welcomed it not as the word of men, but as it is in truth, the word of God, which also effectively works in you who believe.'

Peter places the apostles' writings on the same level with those of the prophets when he says in 2 Peter 3:1, 2: 'Beloved, I now write to you this second epistle (in both of which I stir up your pure minds by way of reminder), that you may be mindful of the words which were spoken before by the holy prophets, and of the commandment of us the apostles of the Lord and Saviour.'

In 1 John 4:6, John says, 'We are of God. He who knows God hears us; he who is not of God does not hear us. By this we know the spirit of truth and the spirit of error.' Ridicule would rest upon anyone outside of the apostolic circle who would dare to make such a claim, but because of the abundant evidence that their teaching originates in God it is immediately accepted and bears witness to its divine origin.

In 2 Peter 3:15 and 16, Peter speaks of the writings of 'our beloved brother Paul'. He says, 'in all his epistles, speaking in them of these things, in which are some things hard to understand, which those who are untaught and unstable twist to their own destruction, as they do also the rest of the Scriptures.' Paul's writings are here placed on an equal level with the Old Testament Scriptures.

It is clearly evident that the apostles knew that they were moving constantly in the realm of divine inspiration and of the impartation of divine knowledge.

Each writer was in a sense left to choose his own words, preserving their individual characteristics. Inspiration allowed personal diligent research as in the case of Luke (Luke 1:1-4).

William Evans states:

'The Spirit employed the attention, the investigation, the memory, the fancy, the logic, in a word, all the faculties of the writer, and wrought through them. He guided the writer to choose the narrative and materials, speeches of others, imperial decrees, genealogies, official letters, state papers or historical matters he might find necessary for the recording of the divine message of salvation. He wrought in, with, and through their spirits, so as to preserve their individuality to others. He used the men themselves and spoke through their individualities. "The gold was His; the mould was theirs."'[13]

From God's side, therefore, He gave to and through His servants truths which He wished to communicate, but from the human side, they communicated those truths in language which they in their individuality would have chosen. God works in and through human freedom. Each writer's character is individually preserved, and each style and type of spiritual understanding is distinct yet parallel.

The Bible is therefore the Word of God in the language of men, altogether divine and yet at the same time altogether human. Infallible guidance was given to the writers to preserve them from error and to write correctly the words of God expressing the ideas which the Holy Spirit intended to convey. God is therefore responsible for every word as it was originally written. We have in our hands, therefore, the divinely inspired communication of God to men.

Chapter 3

ITS ENDORSEMENT BY CHRIST

1. Jesus saw the Old Testament as the Word of God

'The resistless force of our Lord's lightest word makes it imperative that men should appeal to His authority ... with a single intention to learn the truth,' says David MacIntyre.[1] If we know how He regarded Scripture, therefore, we will be forced to believe as He did, for He is the Truth.

His attitude to Scripture was that of trustful obedience. He lived His life according to that which was written for Him in the Book. He bowed His pure will to the revelation of Scripture and obeyed. 'Do not think that I came to destroy the Law or the Prophets. I did not come to destroy but to fulfill,' He said (Matt. 5:17). His life was therefore in harmony with the Scriptures.

Whilst He rebuked Rabbinic glosses on the Law, He nevertheless endorsed the Law; 'The scribes and the Pharisees sit in Moses' seat. Therefore whatever they tell you to observe, that observe and do' (Matt. 23:2 and 3).

It is quite evident that Jesus accepted the Old Testament as authoritative. At His great temptation at the very beginning of His ministry He states three times, '*It is written*,' and then quotes from the Book of Deuteronomy on all three occasions (Matt. 4:4, 7, 10).

He claimed that '*the Scripture cannot be broken*' (John 10:35).

He believed the writers of the Old Testament were inspired by the Holy Spirit. 'For David himself said *by the Holy Spirit*, The LORD said to my Lord ...' (Mark 12:36, quoting from Ps. 110:1).

He speaks of '*the commandment of God*' which the Pharisees had set aside. He then rebuked them saying that they had made 'the *word of God* of no effect through your tradition' (Mark 7:13). He here sets His seal upon the Pentateuch, calling it 'the Word of God'.

In Matthew 5:18, Jesus says, 'Till heaven and earth pass away, one jot or one tittle will by no means pass from the law till all is fulfilled.' The law of Moses is of inviolable divine authority and upon it He sets His seal as an eternal word.

In John 5:47, He asks, 'If you do not believe his (Moses) writings, how will you believe My words?' He identifies with the message of the Pentateuch and stamps His authority on it. This shows the folly of those who will not accept the Pentateuch but do accept the authority of Christ.

When cleansing the temple, He has Isaiah 56:7 as His authority, and said, 'It is written, My house shall be called a house of prayer; but you have made it a den of thieves' (Matt. 21:13.)

When preaching in Nazareth, He read from Isaiah 61:1, 'The Spirit of the LORD is upon Me ...

Today this Scripture is fulfilled in your hearing' (Luke 4:18-21).

He expresses appreciation of the children's praise by quoting *Psalm 8,* and asking the objectors, 'Have you never read, Out of the mouth of babes and nursing infants You have perfected praise?' (Matt. 21:16). What significance in the words, 'Have you never read?' The words are there for them to ponder and accept!

Jesus accepted Old Testament history as true
He believed in the *existence of the patriarchs:* 'Your father Abraham rejoiced to see My day ...' (John 8:56). He quotes from the Old Testament, (Ex. 3: 6), and claims that that 'was spoken to you by God, saying, "I am the God of Abraham, the God of Isaac ..."' (Matt. 22:31, 32). He claims divine authority for the utterance of and also belief in the patriarchs as people, not mere myths.

He accepted the *call of Moses* at the burning bush; 'have you not read in the book of Moses, in the burning bush passage, how God spoke to him ...? (Mark 12:26).

He accepted the *queen of Sheba's visit* to Solomon as historic fact, 'she came from the ends of the earth to hear the wisdom of Solomon' (Luke 11:31).

He accepted the ministry of *the prophet Jonah*, 'For as Jonah became a sign to the Ninevites ... (Luke 11:30).

He acknowledged the murders of *Abel and Zacharias* (Matt. 23:35).

He believed that *David* ate the temple shewbread (Matt. 12:3, 4).

He accepted *Noah* and the flood; 'as it was in the days of Noah, so it will be also in the days of the Son of Man' (Luke 17:26).

He set His seal on the story of *Lot* and the destruction of Sodom (Luke 17:28).

He believed the judgment of *Tyre and Sidon* (Matt. 11:21).

He accepted the ministry of *Elijah and Elisha* and their miracles, and acknowledged the existence of *Naaman* (Luke 4:25-27).

He accepted the *ministry of Moses* in the wilderness, 'As Moses lifted up the serpent in the wilderness' (John 3:14).

Jesus accepted Old Testament prophecy as true
He acknowledged John as prophet and forerunner; 'A prophet? Yes, I say to you, and more than a prophet' (Matt. 11:9), accepting the prophecy of *Malachi* in this regard (3:1).

He accepted *Isaiah's* prophecy; 'Well did Isaiah prophesy of you hypocrites ...' (Mk. 7:6 quoting Is. 29:13).

He quotes the prophet *Zechariah* (13:7), when speaking of His death in Matthew 26:31, 'I will strike the Shepherd, and the sheep of the flock will be scattered.'

In Luke 22:37, He tells them that the words of *Isaiah 53:12* are to be fulfilled in Himself; 'He was numbered with the transgressors.'

In John 13:18, He tells them that the words of *Psalm 41:9* are to be fulfilled in the case of the traitor; 'He who eats bread with Me has lifted up his heel against Me.'

He speaks of 'the abomination of desolation, spoken of by *Daniel* the prophet' (Matt. 24:15). So Daniel was not a figment of the imagination but a real person.

On the Cross He uses the opening and closing words of *Psalm 22*, 'My God, My God, why have You forsaken Me' (Matt. 27:46), and, 'It is finished' (John 19:30), and the words of *Psalm 31:5* 'Into Your hands I commend My Spirit' (Luke 23:46).

Jesus said, 'The Son of Man goes as it is written of Him ...' (Matt. 26:24); and again, 'this which is written must still be accomplished in Me' (Luke 22:37).

When they arrested Him in Gethsemane, Jesus said, 'Have you come out, as against a robber, with swords and clubs to take Me? ... But all this was done that the Scriptures of the prophets might be fulfilled' (Matt. 26:55, 56).

To the Jews He said, 'You search the Scriptures, for in them you think you have eternal life; and these are they which testify of Me' (John 5:39). He recognized that the Old Testament Scriptures focused upon Him. There is an unbreakable link between the predictions, prophecies and pictures of the Old Testament and the fulfilment of those statements and figures in Him. His life miraculously unites and endorses the various strands of thought written by so many different people over a period of more than 1000 years and gathered together in the body of writings which we call the Old Testament Scriptures.

It will be seen that Jesus lived in the light of Scripture. He was directed by it, He revered its teaching, acknowledged its authority, knew of its divine origin. Jesus was a Man of the Book.

After His resurrection in Luke 24, we read, 'beginning at Moses and all the Prophets, He expounded to them in all the Scriptures the things concerning Himself' (v. 27). In verse 44, He says, 'All things must be fulfilled which were written in the Law of Moses and *the* Prophets and *the* Psalms concerning Me.' He sets His seal on all three sections of the Old Testament, the Law, the Prophets and the Writings. He does this after His resurrection, indicating that He was not subject to the limitations and ignorance of the age in which He had lived. It has been said that He merely reflected the delusions and theological misconceptions of Israelite thinking when He accepted the Old Testament so literally, but this argument is dispelled by the fact that He is speaking from beyond the grave, beyond the thought-patterns of His Judean society and culture.

In addition, He is 'the Truth' (John 14:6). He is 'the Amen, the Faithful and True Witness' (Rev. 3:14). If He were to endorse as true that which was false, He would not be 'the Truth' at all. As 'Truth' however, He cannot endorse falsehood. If He as Truth endorses the Old Testament Scriptures, then it must follow that His endorsement is true and that the Scriptures are reliable and authoritative. To accept the authority of Jesus and not to accept the authority of the Bible is illogical. If we accept the authority of Jesus we must accept the Bible as the Word of God, for Jesus endorses it as such.

Jesus warns us that those who indulge in denials of the trustworthiness of the earlier Scriptures, will eventually find themselves rejecting His authority: 'For if you believed Moses, you would believe Me; for he wrote about Me. But if you do not believe his writings, how will you believe My words?' (John 5:46, 47). How true of our own day.

Jesus then accepted the Old Testament Scriptures at their face value, holding them to be completely truthful and reliable. He nourished His own spiritual life and resisted the devil through the Scriptures. He endured suffering, discouragement and death, fulfilling what the Scriptures said was in store for Him, because of His trust in the Scriptures. He claimed that these Scriptures were so inspired that they should be spoken of as 'the Word of God'. His utterances concerning the Scriptures are final and authoritative. He showed that the Scriptures are divine truth and had infallible authority.

Well did Bishop Moule state:

'The New Testament as a whole is a mass of valid historical evidence to the opinions of Jesus Christ, and in this character it attests beyond a doubt His profound veneration for the Holy Scriptures then existing; that is to say, for the Old Testament as, in substance and practically in detail it exists today. For

Him it possessed the peculiar and awful characteristic of divine authority. He stated no theory of its construction, but, looking upon it as it existed, He recognized in it the decisive utterance of God, even in its minor features of expression. For the mind which recognizes in Jesus Christ all that He claimed to be, this verdict on the supernatural character and divine authority of the Old Testament is final.'[2]

It is clear therefore that if we accept Christ, we accept the Bible. Christ and the Bible stand or fall together. Anyone who makes any part of the Bible a lie, makes Jesus Christ a liar. Jesus quoted and believed the Old Testament and placed His authority and guarantee upon its authenticity and authority.

2. Jesus' View of His Own Words

Jesus was completely confident that His words were authoritative, vital and true. He said:

'Heaven and earth will pass away, but My words will by no means pass away' (Mark 13:31);

'If you abide in My word ... you shall know the truth, and the truth shall make you free' (John 8:31-32).

'Jesus answered them and said, My doctrine is not mine, but His who sent Me' (John 7:16).

'For I have not spoken on My own *authority*; but the Father who sent Me gave Me a command, what I should say and what I should speak' (John 12:49).

'The words that I speak to you are spirit, and *they* are life' (John 6:63).

'He who hears My word and believes in Him who sent Me has everlasting life' (John 5:24).

'You are already clean because of the word which I have spoken to you' (John 15:3).

He knew that His words were eternal. They were authoritative; they were divine. He realized that He was the expression and revelation of the Father. He was the Word, the Logos, the extension of the Father's being. The Father had spoken in the Old Testament through the prophets, and was now speaking through Him. He was the Alpha and Omega (the first and last letters of the Greek alphabet). All that the Father wanted to say to mankind, He now said in Christ. He was God's Word to humanity, and the words which He spoke reflected the eternity from which He came. 'No man ever spoke like this Man' (John 7:46). 'In the beginning was the Word ... and the Word became flesh' (John 1:1, 14). He was the personified Word of the Father. God spoke in Him, so His spoken words were the outflow of the living divine union. The 'Word was with God, and the Word was God' (John 1:1). The words of Jesus came from heaven itself. That is why He could say, 'My words shall never pass away.'

3. Jesus' View of the Words of Those who Followed Him

In John 16:12 and 13, Jesus said, 'I still have many things to say to you, but you cannot bear *them* now. However, when He, the Spirit of truth, has come,

He will guide you into all truth ...'

He is saying that whilst they were not yet ready to receive the teaching which He could give, the Spirit would later lead them into all truth. The teaching of the apostles would be as true as His own, in fact theirs would be a fuller revelation than He had been able to impart because of their impenetrable hearts. He had to keep back many things because they were not ready for them. The Apostles would not be left to their fallible memories, but the Holy Spirit would bring truth to their minds and the revelation which they would give would be owned and guided by the Spirit, an even fuller testimony to truth.

Knowing beforehand the contents of their message, He gave their words the same authority as His: 'Whoever will not receive you nor hear your words ... shake off the dust from your feet' (Matt. 10:14). 'He who hears you hears Me ...' (Luke 10:16).

We cannot forget His great statement, 'I have given to them the words which You have given Me' (John 17:8). He endorsed the message which was to follow.

He assures them that it would be given them what they were to speak. He says, 'whatever is given you ... speak that; for it is not you who speak, but the Holy Spirit' (Mark 13:11). In Matthew 10:20, He says that it is 'the Spirit of your Father who speaks in you.' The Holy Spirit is here identified with the Spirit of the Father indicating the oneness of the Trinity.

Amid all the differences of understanding, culture and training of those who were to preach the Word, there is a remarkable harmony which can only be explained by the fact that, 'the Lord gave the Word; great was the company of those who proclaimed it' (Ps. 68:11).

Chapter 4

ITS PROPHECY

Biblical prophecy and its fulfilment is an extremely large subject but it is possible nevertheless to show briefly the general impact of the argument.

The Scriptures were rigorous in their test of a prophet: 'When a prophet speaks in the name of the LORD, if the thing does not happen or come to pass, that is the thing which the LORD has not spoken' (Deut. 18:22). In fact if the guidance from the prophet did not accord with God's will, 'that prophet or that dreamer of dreams shall be put to death' (Deut. 13:5).

A prophet is one who receives truth from God and who conveys this truth to his fellow man. He is a spokesman of God to men, receiving his instructions by the agency of the Holy Spirit. He is conscious of his high calling and acts under divine constraint. He represents Jehovah to the people and is therefore fearless and authoritative in his proclamations.

Many have denied that prophets predict future events saying that prophecy mongering is intellectually ruinous and that the prophets must have lived in the period which they describe. These critics fail to acknowledge that hundreds of predictions in the Old Testament have already become history; and in particular the writings of the Old Testament, which spoke so clearly of Christ, could not have been written at the time of Christ. Their claims, and denials of the supernatural are not worthy of consideration.

The harmony of the prophets is something which is truly remarkable. These men came from a variety of backgrounds, they had differing intellectual abilities and social standing, they were separated from one another by centuries, and yet their message is one. How, if not by the operation of the Spirit of God, is this to be explained? On a human level it would be utterly impossible, but if they were led by God's Spirit, He would bring the same message through all of them throughout the 1000 years of written prophecy.

Fulfilled prophecy is a fact which every thinking person must face and acknowledge. Many Old Testament prophecies were plain, minute and explicit and have been fulfilled to the very letter. Prophecies at times looked ahead only a few years, but had in addition a future fulfilment as well.

1. The Prophetic Nature of Its Statements
There are three lines of prophecy in the Old Testament, prophecies about the Gentiles, prophecies about Israel and prophecies about the Messiah.

1. Gentile Prophecies
There are numerous prophecies relating to the smaller nations around Israel such as the Philistines,

the Edomites, the Moabites and the Syrians, which have long since been fulfilled. Nahum prophesied the destruction of Nineveh.

One outstanding illustration of prophecy concerning the Gentiles is found in Daniel 2 where Daniel describes the great image in the dream of Nebuchadnezzar. The golden head represented Babylon, the breast of silver the Medo-Persian empire, the brass thighs and stomach the Greek empire; the iron legs and feet the Roman empire, and the stone which struck the image the spiritual kingdom which God Himself set up in which we now live.

2. Prophecies concerning Israel

Many prophecies concerning Israel have been fulfilled with meticulous accuracy.

In Leviticus 26:31-33, we read: 'I will lay your cities waste, and bring your sanctuaries to desolation, and I will not smell the fragrance of your sweet aromas. I will bring the land to desolation; and your enemies who dwell in it shall be astonished at it. I will scatter you among the nations and draw out a sword after you; your land shall be desolate, and your cities waste.' This prophecy was given before they entered Canaan but it assumes that they would, which they did. The subsequent predictions also literally came to pass.

When Ahab and Jehoshaphat were about to go to war against Syria, the prophet Micaiah prophesied that Israel would be defeated and Ahab

61

killed: 'I saw all Israel scattered on the mountains, as sheep that have no shepherd. And the LORD said, These have no master ... ' (1 Kings 22:17). For his courage and honesty he was jailed (v. 27), but the king died that day and was buried in Samaria (v. 37). This was a short-term prophecy that found immediate fulfilment.

Jeremiah predicted the Babylonian captivity: 'And this whole land shall be a desolation *and* an astonishment, and these nations shall serve the king of Babylon seventy years' (Jer. 25:11).

Isaiah, who lived 740-680 BC, made many predictions, one of which also concerns Babylon: 'Behold, the days are coming when all that is in your house, and what your fathers have accumulated until this day, shall be carried to Babylon' (Is. 39:6). This was made more than 100 years before it happened.

Ezekiel prophesied Israel's return, 'For I will take you from among the nations, gather you out of all countries, and bring you into your own land' (Ezek. 36:24). This prophecy not only speaks to Israel's immediate condition, but in the long term it was fulfilled when Israel returned from its world-wide dispersion and became a nation once more in 1948.

Amos, an eighth century prophet prophesying in the reign of Jeroboam II in Israel, and Uzziah in Judah in about the year 787 BC, predicted the dispersion and restoration of Israel: 'On that day I will raise up the tabernacle of David, which has fallen down, and repair its damages; I will raise up its ruins, and rebuild it as in the days of old ... and they shall build the waste cities, and inhabit *them*' (Amos 9:11-15).

These prophecies and their fulfilment make convincing reading. Surely, then, the Lord spoke through the prophets and the word must be His.

3. *Messianic Prophecies*
Scroggie claims that 'there are at least 300 of these traceable, many of which were fulfilled by Christ's first advent, and the remainder shall be fulfilled at His second advent.'[1] Nowhere is the evidence of genuine prediction more evident than in the Old Testament passages which speak of the Messiah. Two portraits of the Messiah emerge, that of a kingly Messiah and that of a suffering Messiah. Some rabbinic scholars thought that there could well be two Messiahs, a political and a spiritual one.

Kevin Connor has listed some of the prophecies and their fulfilment and I quote his list below:

The Prophecy	The Fulfilment
1. Seed of the Woman: Gen. 3:15	Gal. 4:4
2. Of the line of Shem: Gen. 9:26	Luke 3:36
3. Seed of Abraham: Gen. 22:18	Matt. 1:1
4. Seed of Isaac: Gen. 26:2-4	Luke 3:34
5. Seed of Jacob: Gen. 28:13-14, Num. 24:17-19	Luke 3:34
6. Of the Nation of Israel: Deut. 18:18	Rom. 9:4-5
7. Of the Tribe of Judah: Gen. 49:10-12	Heb. 7:14, Rev. 5:5
8. Of the Family of Jesse: Is. 11:1-2	Matt. 1:6
9. Of the House of David: 2 Sam. 7:12-14	Rom. 1:2-3, Matt. 9:27, Matt. 1:1

63

10. David's Lord, David's Son: Ps. 110:1	Rev. 22:16, Matt. 22:41-46
11. Born of a Virgin: Is. 7:14, Jer. 31:22	Matt. 1:18-23
12. Created a New Thing: Jer. 31:22	Luke 1:34-35
13. The Mighty God: Is. 9:6-7	John 1:1-3, 14, I Tim. 3:16
14. The Son Begotten: Ps. 2:7, 12	John 3:16, Matt. 3:17
15. The Son's Name: Prov. 30:4	Matt. 1:21
16. To inherit Throne of David: Is. 9:6-7	Luke 1:31-33
17. To be born at Bethlehem: Micah 5:2	Matt. 2:1-8
18. Slaughter of innocents: Jer. 31:15	Matt. 2:16-18
19. The Star of Messiah: Num. 24:17	Matt. 2:1-2, 9-10
20. Out of Egypt: Hosea 11:1	Matt. 2:12-15
21. Messiah's Forerunner: Is. 40:3, Mal. 3:1	Matt. 3:1, 2, 3
22. To be manifested after 483 years: Dan. 9:25	Mark 1:15
23. Messiah's Anointing: Is. 61:1-4, Ps. 45:7	Luke 4:16-22, Acts 10:38
24. The fullness of the Spirit: Is. 11:1-4	John 3:34, Rev. 5:6
25. Ministry for 3 1/2 years: Dan. 9:24-27	The 4 Gospels
26. To be 30 years of age: Num. 4:3	Luke 3:23
27. Ministry in Galilee, Is. 9:1-2, 8	Matt. 4:12-16, Luke 4:14
28. The Prophet like unto Moses: Deut. 18:18	Acts 3:19-26, John 6:14
29. To be a King and Law-Giver: Gen. 49:10	Matt. 5, 6, 7 (Laws of Kingdom)
30. The Shepherd-Stone: Gen. 49:24	John 10:11, Matt. 21:42-45
31. His zeal for God: Ps. 69:9	John 2:13-17
32. Must come to the Temple: Mal. 3:1	Matt. 21:12-15, Luke 2:25-32
33. Ministry of miracles, healings: Is. 35	Matt. 8, Matt. 11:4-5
34. To come in the Name of the Lord: Ps. 118:26	Matt. 21:9-11

35. Gracious in word: Ps. 45:2	John 1:17, Luke 4:22
36. Speak God's Word by commandment: Deut. 18:18	John 8:28, 38, John 12:47-50
37. To speak in Name of God: Deut. 18:19	John 5:43
38. To speak in parables: Ps. 78:1-4	Matt. 13:3-35
39. Half-brothers reject Him: Ps. 69:8	John 1:11, John 7:1-5
40. Rejected by leaders: Ps. 118:22	Acts 4:1-12, Matt. 21:42-45
41. Not many believe: Is. 53:1	John 12:37-38
42. Spiritual blindness: Is. 6:9, 29:13	John 12:39-41, Matt. 13:14
43. Messiah to be 'cut off' after 3 1/2 years: Dan. 9:26	Mark 15:25
44. To be cut off for our sins: Is. 53:8	2 Cor. 5:21
45. Make reconciliation: Dan. 9:24	2 Cor. 5:18-21
46. Sold for 30 pieces of silver: Zech. 11:13	Matt. 27:3-4, Matt. 26:14-16
47. Silver cast down in Lord's House: Zech. 11:13	Matt. 27:5
48. To the Potter: Zech. 11:13	Matt. 27:6-10
49. Ride on ass into city: Zech. 9:9, Gen. 49:11	John 12:12-16, Matt. 21:1-11
50. Betrayed by a friend: Ps. 41:9	John 13:18-21
51. False witnesses accuse: Ps. 35:11	Matt. 26:60-61, Mark 14:55-65
52. Dumb as a Lamb before accusers. Is. 53:7	Matt. 26:63, 27:12-14, Acts 8:32
53. Smitten and spat upon: Is. 50:6	Matt. 26:67-68, John 18:22
54. Cheek smitten, hair plucked: Is. 50:6, Micah 5:1	Luke 22:63-64
55. Stripes of Law: Deut. 25:1-3, Is. 53:5	John 19:1, I Pet. 2:24
56. Cursed to hang on a tree: Deut. 21:23	Gal. 3:10, 13, I Pet. 2:24

57. Back as a plowed field: Ps. 129:3	Mark 15:15-17
58. Despised, rejected of men: Is. 53:3	I Pet. 2:3-8
59. Man of Sorrows: Is. 53:3, Lam. 1:12	Luke 23:27-31, Luke 19:41
60. Visage marred, and form: Is. 52:14, Is. 53:2	John 19:1-5
61. Forsaken by disciples: Zech. 13:7	Matt. 26:30-31
62. In prison and judgement: Is. 53:8	John 18:28
63. Hated without a cause: Ps. 69:4, Ps. 109:2-5	John 15:23-25
64. Forsaken of God: Ps. 22:1	Matt. 27:46
65. A reproach of men: Ps. 22:6, 69:9	Rom. 15:1-3, Heb. 13:13
66. A broken heart: Ps. 69:20, 22:14	John 19:34-37
67. Given gall and vinegar in thirst: Ps. 69:21	John 19:29, Matt. 27:34-48
68. Shake their heads at Him: Ps. 22:7-8, 109:25	Matt. 27:39
69. Bones out of joint: Ps. 22:14, 17	Crucifixion on the Cross
70. To be stared at: Ps. 22:17	Matt. 27:36, Luke 23:35
71. Hands and feet pierced: Ps. 22:16, Zech. 13:6	John 20:27, 19:18, 37, Luke 23:33
72. Side to be pierced: Zech. 12:10	John 19:34, Rev. 1:7
73. Blood and water cleansings: Lev. 14:4-6	John 19:34-36
74. Parted His garments: Ps. 22:18	John 19:23, Mark 15:24
75. Cast lots for His vesture: Ps. 22:18	John 19:23-24, Matt. 27:35
76. Not a bone to be broken: Ex. 12:46, Ps. 34:20	John 19:33-36
77. Prays for enemies: Ps. 109:4, Is. 53:12	Luke 23:34
78. Numbered with transgressors: Is. 53:12	Mark 15:27-28

79. Sun to go down at noon: Amos 8:9-10	Matt. 27:45
80. At even, going down of Sun: Deut. 16:6	Mark 15:33-34, 42
81. Carried own wood: Gen. 22:9	John 19:17-18, Matt. 27:31-32
82. Commits spirit to God: Ps. 31:5	Luke 23:46
83. Sins of world laid on Him: Is. 53:4-12	2 Cor. 5:18-21, 1 Pet. 2:24
84. Burial with the rich: Is. 53:9	Matt. 27:57-60
85. Bruised the serpent's head: Gen. 3:15	Heb. 2:11, 14-15, Rom. 16:20
86. Bruised by the serpent: Gen. 3:15	Matt. 16:21-24
87. Bruised by the Lord: Is. 53:10	Acts 2:23, 3:18
88. Buried for 3 days and nights: Jonah 1:17	Matt. 12:39-40, 1 Cor. 15:1-4
89. Body not see corruption: Ps. 16:10	Acts 13:35, 2:24-32
90. Ascends on high, gives gifts: Ps. 68:18	Eph. 4:8-16
91. Sits on right hand of God: Ps. 110:1	Heb. 1:3
92. Exalted King-Priest: Is. 52:13, Ps. 110:1-4, Zech. 6:12-13	Mark 16:19,

Such an array of prophecies given by so many prophets over such a long time being fulfilled in one person within a few years, and most of them in one day, is an impressive proof that the prophets were inspired when they wrote.[2]

2. The Prophetic Nature of its History and Characters

Bishop Westcott states: 'the whole history is prophetic. It is not enough to recognise that the Old Testament contains prophecies: the Old Testament is one vast prophecy.'[3]

Not only are Isaiah, Jeremiah, Daniel and the other writers prophets, but the recorded lives of the patriarchs and several Old Testament characters are prophetic in their historical setting.

1. Its History

The journey from Egypt to Canaan is a classic example. The history of the Israelites pictures the New Testament plan of salvation showing that the Old Testament and the New Testament present one message. In the Old Testament it is the shadows and types, and in the New Testament we have the reality of an accomplished salvation.

The Israelites were in bondage to the Egyptians. Egypt is a picture of the old life of sin in which all are held under the domination of Pharaoh, who represents the devil. The only way to be rescued from Egypt's bondage and God's judgement was through the blood of the lamb. They were to be spared from the judgement of God, which rested on the whole land, only by applying the blood to their doorposts. This, of course, is a picture of God's judgement on the sinful world, from which we can escape solely by applying the blood of the Lamb of God to our hearts. The judgement passed from the people to the lamb. The slain lamb is the substitute for the first-born, and God's Lamb is our substitute. He dies in our place, and we are free from the old life of bondage, sorrow and sin through the blood of the Lamb.

On their journey they were immediately fed on

manna from heaven, a picture of Jesus nourishing His people, as He Himself explains when they said to Him: 'Our fathers ate the manna in the desert; as it is written, He gave them bread from heaven to eat. Then Jesus said to them, Most assuredly, I say to you, Moses did not give you the bread from heaven, but My Father gives you the true bread from heaven. For the bread of God is He who comes down from heaven and gives life unto the world ... I am the bread of life' (John 6:31-35).

They needed water, and when Moses struck the rock the water flowed for all to quench their thirst. Paul tells us that 'they drank of that spiritual Rock ... and that Rock was Christ' (1 Cor. 10:4). Later when they again needed water, God instructed Moses to speak to the rock and water would gush out. In his impetuosity Moses struck the rock twice and 'the water came out abundantly'. But Moses had spoiled the type. Jesus was only smitten once, thereafter men need only speak to Him to know the gracious flow of blessing. Because of this hasty action Moses was denied the privilege of taking the children of Israel into the promised land (Num. 20:8-12).

In their discouragement the people spoke against God, who then sent poisonous snakes among the people, and many died. 'We have sinned,' they said, and God told Moses to make a brass snake and put it on a pole. When the people who had been bitten looked at the brass snake, the poison was nullified and they lived. This prophetic action was fulfilled in Jesus who said, 'as Moses lifted up the serpent in the wilderness, even so must the Son of Man be lifted up, that whoever believes in Him should not perish but have eternal life' (John 3:14 and 15).

Their eventful journey from Egypt had one objective, to bring them to Canaan; 'Then He brought us out from there, that He might bring us in, to give us the land of which He swore to our fathers' (Deut. 6:23). As many able commentators have affirmed, the picture of Canaan is that of a life of Christian victory and fullness, blessing and fruitfulness, of rest and stability, of holiness and beauty, of service and purpose. The exhortations in Hebrews chapters 3 and 4 to enter into that rest that is provided for the people of God are far more appropriate when applied to the life of Christian fullness and blessing than to heaven, which it also undoubtedly pictures, for they ate from the manna until they crossed over Jordan.

2. Its Characters

Abraham and Isaac are clear Old Testament types of New Testament truths. Like Jesus, Isaac was born contrary to the laws of nature. Isaac was mocked by his brother (Gen. 21:9), and Jesus was rejected by the Jews. Isaac was the sole heir of all that his father possessed (Gen. 24:36), and Jesus is 'appointed heir of all things' (Heb. 1:2.)

Abraham and Isaac walked up the hill of sacrifice with Isaac carrying the wood upon which he was to die (Gen. 22:6), a picture of Calvary, where Jesus carried the Cross. Abraham, the father, was to kill his beloved son. Of Jesus it is written that he was 'stricken, smitten of God ...' (Is. 53). God, the Father, smote His beloved Son. Isaac rose from this virtual death and entered into his inheritance. When Jesus rose from the dead all the riches of heaven were His. This whole story is a beautiful picture of the sacrificing Father and the submissive Son. The ram caught in the thicket and sacrificed instead of Isaac is another aspect of the substitutionary death of Christ.

Joseph is an enthralling picture of Christ. He, the first-born son of Rachel, was sent on a long journey by his father to his brothers, who, on his arrival, held him prisoner and then sold him to foreigners for twenty pieces of silver. Jesus, the first-born, came all the way from heaven to earth to His own people, but they did not receive Him (John 1:11). Instead they rejected Him, selling Him for thirty pieces of silver and handing Him over to a foreign power to be crucified.

Joseph died figuratively in the prisons of Egypt but eventually returned as the conquering ruler, with a plan of salvation for all the starving multitudes of the world. There was food enough to feed them all. Although he had disappeared from public view, having been wrongly accused, he returned as the saviour of the world. Jesus too was wrongly accused and put to death, but He returned from the dead with a plan of salvation that has been published to the ends of the earth. He is the mighty Saviour of all who will come and receive the salvation He offers. He brings life and health to the starving multitudes of earth.

Moses is a picture of Christ, for immediately after his birth the evil rulers sought to kill him. He escaped but they killed many other little boys at that time. Mary and Joseph fled with their precious child to Egypt whilst the slaughter of the innocent children took place in Israel (Matt. 2:16-18).

He instituted the Passover (Ex. 12:14-28), that wonderful picture of Calvary where the blood of the lamb was struck on the doorposts of Israelite homes, saving them from the wrath of Yahweh. The lamb was the substitute for their first-born. The New Testament affirms, 'Christ, our Passover, was sacrificed for us' (1 Cor. 5:7). He was our substitute Lamb.

Moses became the wonderful leader, saving them from the yoke of bondage in Egypt and leading them out on an untried way. Delivered from the old life of slavery, they now had to depend on God for their very existence. There was no food in the desert. It had to come from heaven, and on that heavenly food they lived. Jesus saves from Satan's cruel bondage, separating us from the old life of sorrow and sin and leading us out in the wilderness of this world where there is no food for the soul. He is our very life, for we live in Him and feed on Him, the heavenly Manna, the living Bread.

72

Joshua was the great leader and conqueror of the land of Canaan. He took them over the Jordan and led them in their central, southern and northern campaigns until the land was subdued. He brought them peace and stability instead of their restless wanderings in the wilderness – again a picture of Christ leading us to a life of victory and rest.

David the shepherd boy became Israel's greatest king. He killed Goliath with one of his five chosen stones. When Jesus was tempted by the devil, He quoted three times from Deuteronomy, one of the five books of Moses, and emerged victorious from the temptation.

When David finally came to the throne he looked for those of the house of Saul that he might show them kindness 'for Jonathan's sake' (2 Sam. 9). Mephibosheth was found and he ate at David's table continually in Jerusalem. God shows us kindness for Jesus' sake and accepts us into His family where we partake of the delicacies of heaven in the presence of the King.

When David was established as king, Absalom his son conspired against him, eventually overthrowing him and driving him into the wilderness. In this rebellion, David was betrayed by those in his inner circle. Ahithophel, David's influential counsellor (2 Sam. 15:12), and wonderful friend, (Ps. 55:12-14, 21), became one of the conspirators and joined the revolt. His later counsel to Absalom was not followed, and, in sorrow of heart, he hanged himself (2 Sam. 17:23). Jesus too was betrayed by one in the inner circle. Zechariah, in his prophecy, asks about the wounds in his hands, and receives the reply that they are 'those with which I was wounded in the house of my friends' (Zech. 13:6). Judas Iscariot was one of Christ's closest associates on earth and he betrayed Him. He too, like Ahithophel, was filled with sorrow, and in remorse he hanged himself (Matt. 27:5).

Above all, David was the warrior king who subdued all his enemies and brought peace to the land, a wonderful picture of our all-conquering Lord. David's sure trust and close relationship with God is woven into all his writings. The Psalms breathe an intimacy of communion with the Lord. Jesus too enjoyed that closeness and oneness with the Father.

David the king was rejected by his own family. He was the king in rejection, but he returned and brought untold blessings to his people. Jesus was also rejected by His own people but returned to reign and rule, and bring eternal blessings to those who trust in Him.

Solomon instituted the brightest age of Israel's history. It was Israel's golden age when the nation rose to its highest fame and achieved its greatest influence, extending its borders to the furthest limits.

It is a picture of Christ in His great glory. Even Solomon's 1000 wives mirror the great bride of Christ in the time of His glorious rule and triumph.

Daniel was numbered with those who were well-favoured, who were of the king's family and of the princes (Dan. 1:3). He was carried, nevertheless, into captivity and in Babylon was hidden from the position of power and poise which would normally have been his in his own land. He was royalty or aristocracy in obscurity. Like Joseph, from a position of 'death' he rose to be the greatest in the land, and as prime minister brought great blessing to the nations over which he ruled. His character and conduct were blameless, his dedication to God's plan and will whatever the consequences, even certain death in the lions' den, was obvious. His prayerful intimacy with heaven was open for all to see. In all these things he pictures Christ, who came from heaven's glory and was hidden in obscurity in Nazareth, was put to death on Calvary, but rose as the mighty Conqueror, and now rules, bringing blessing to all.

Old Testament characters and events picture New Testament truths and are prophetic in their nature and history.

3. The Prophetic Nature of its Religion

1. The Tabernacle and the Temple
'God is a Spirit, – infinite, eternal and unchangeable, – in His being, wisdom, power, holiness, justice, goodness and truth' (Shorter Catechism).

How is this incomparable Being, so Wholly Other, to communicate with insignificant man?

In His infinite wisdom God became man. He projected Himself into the human race in the person of His Son, Jesus Christ. Jesus was a man as other men, but 'God was in Christ' (2 Cor. 5:19). Within that visible human form dwelt Almighty God. This is pictured for us in the Old Testament.

In the book of Exodus we read how the Israelites journeyed from Egypt to Canaan. On the journey they constructed a tabernacle where God dwelt among His people. It was erected in the centre of the camp. The outward covering was of badger skins.

If one were to gaze across the camp of Israel it would not be all that significant simply because it resembled all the other tents surrounding it. It may have stood in its own enclosure, but there was nothing there to strike awe into one's heart. It was just another tent, and, like the other tents, would be covered with the dust of the desert. Just so Jesus was just another man – a man like other men, without any significant physical characteristic or noteworthy difference, but – 'God was in Christ!'

In the desert the great significance lay *within* the Tabernacle. Beneath the badger skins were the coverings of rams' skins dyed red, signifying Christ's death. Beneath the rams' skins were the curtains of goats' hair, speaking of the prophets' clothing, and signifying Christ's prophetic role. Beneath the goats' hair were the beautiful curtains of fine twined linen, signifying Christ's righteousness – embroidered with blue (His heavenly character), purple (His regal character), and red (His earthly character).

In the Holy Place was the Table of Shewbread ('I am the bread of life' – John 6:48), the Golden Candlestick ('I am the light of the world' – John 8:12), and the Golden Altar of incense ('He ever lives to make intercession for them' – Heb. 7:25).

In the Holiest of all was the Ark – a box made of shittim wood, signifying Christ's humanity, and completely covered with gold, speaking of His deity, and all beautifully blended in one unit. Here we have typified the deity and manhood of Jesus Christ. 'God was manifested in the flesh' (I Tim. 3:16). God and man – one Christ, one glorious Person, is presented to us here. The wood and the gold were *moulded* together. At the heart of the place where God met with man is a revelation of the incarnation. God deigned to identify with man by actually uniting with him in this intensely intricate, personal and mysterious way. God and man blended together in Jesus Christ. 'God was in Christ.'

The Ark was covered by the Mercy Seat, which was a slab of pure gold. It formed the lid of the Ark. Only once a year the high priest entered the Holy of Holies to make atonement for the sins of the people. When he did so, on the Day of Atonement, he sprinkled blood on that gold slab. The blood from the earth trickled on to the gold, which represented deity. Again there is this strange and marvellous union. This is where God meets

77

man! 'There I will meet with you' (Ex. 25:17-22). Here is Christ's sacrifice. Here is God in Christ shedding His precious blood as an offering for our sins. Here is Calvary.

Here, then, is the Incarnation and the Crucifixion typified in one item of furniture – the Ark. It is here, in Christ typified, that God meets man. His incarnation and His crucifixion are inextricably linked together. Bethlehem and Calvary are inseparable.

In the Ark were three things:

1. The golden pot containing manna – a picture of Christ's life and provision for His people.
2. The tables of the Covenant with the Ten Commandments, which Christ alone kept perfectly.
3. Aaron's rod that budded, a picture of Christ's resurrection.

The Veil of blue, purple and red, separating the Holy Place and the Holy of Holies illustrates again in its three colours, the Divinity, Kingship and Humanity of Christ. The veil was His flesh (Heb. 10:20). When Christ died, God rent the veil from top to bottom. He was 'smitten of God'. 'It pleased the Lord to bruise Him' (Is. 53:4, 10). When the veil was torn asunder, the way into the Holy of Holies stood wide open. Man could now enter God's presence. When Jesus died, He became the way to God. Through His rent body, through His death, the way into the presence of God was at last open.

We have access through Christ's death into the very presence of God.

Therefore, whilst the external appearance of the Tabernacle was merely that of a tent (the humanity of Christ disguises His deity), inside, the glory of God and His marvellous plan of salvation were portrayed. It spoke of the Incarnation, of the Crucifixion, of God meeting man in Christ. Only in Jesus Christ does God meet man, and the Tabernacle is a beautiful type of His person and work.

2. In The Offerings

The system of the Levitical priesthood and its offerings is described in Leviticus 1 – 7. There are five offerings; the first three are called sweet-savour offerings, and the last two, non sweet-savour offerings. The first three typify Christ in His perfection and devotion to the will of God. They are the Whole Burnt Offering, the Meal Offering and the Peace Offering. The last two are the Sin Offering and the Trespass Offering, and typify Christ as bearing the failure, sin and punishment of the sinner.

The Burnt Offering. The offerings of a bullock, a lamb, a goat or a pigeon were to be without blemish and offered voluntarily. Jesus offered Himself voluntarily 'without spot' (Heb. 9:14). All the offering was burnt upon the altar (Lev. 1:9). Not a piece was retained. Jesus gave Himself unreservedly and completely.

The Meal Offering. This presents Christ in His perfect humanity and as such is a bloodless offering. The ingredients required were:

a. Fine flour. He, the corn of wheat produced the fine flour and declared, 'I am the bread of life.'

b. Oil was mingled with the offering and was also poured on it. Oil speaks of the Holy Spirit. He was conceived by the Holy Spirit and also anointed by the Spirit. (Acts 10:38)

c. Frankincense when burned on the altar released a sweet-smelling fragrance. Christ's life of sacrifice was fragrant to God and man.

d. Salt has cleansing properties. It flavours and it preserves. No leaven or honey was included; leaven indicating evil and honey speaking of natural goodness and glory. The glory was of God and for God. The beautiful, balanced and blameless life of Christ is typified in this offering.

The Peace Offering. As the whole burnt offering depicts Christ's yieldedness to His Father's will, and as the meal offering presents His blameless life, so the peace offering follows with His death upon Calvary. The offering was to be without blemish, and Christ, who was the only one without blemish, is the only one whom the law would not condemn, and who consequently could make an acceptable sacrifice, thus securing peace. The bullock, lamb or goat without blemish was offered. Christ had no blemish in His person, character, or life. On that ground He was accepted. The Hebrew worshipper shall 'lay his hand on the head of his offering' (Lev. 3:2). The lamb is his offering, and the symbolic act of laying his hand upon the head of the offering is a solemn, sacred and significant act of identification. Christ is our Lamb. We acknowledge personal guilt, accept the divine sentence, identify with His death and appropriate all the benefits secured by Him.

The Sin Offering. The bullock, kid or lamb without blemish is selected. The worshipper lays his hand upon the head of the offering, indicating the transference of sin from the sinner to the substitute. In this offering it is the person, the sinner himself who is in view, and the offering atones for his sin. The carcass of the bullock was taken outside the camp and burned there. Calvary was outside the city. God made Jesus 'who knew no sin *to be* sin for us' (2 Cor. 5:21). He is our sin-offering. The priest makes an atonement for the sinner, and 'it shall be forgiven them' (Lev. 4:20). Forgiveness is pronounced. God pronounces forgiveness on all those who trust in His great Sin-offering, Jesus Christ. The Old Testament offering typifies God's great offering of His Son Jesus Christ, on Calvary, outside the city. He is 'the Lamb ' (John 1:29).

The Trespass Offering. Here, atonement is made for our sinful acts. It is the trespass, the deed, the act against God and against man that is in view. The transgressor makes an offering, the priest makes atonement and God assures forgiveness.

81

These offerings were ingrained in the life of every Israelite. The system was instituted when Israel left Egypt in about 1440 BC. Century after century passed and the offerings were still being made. The nation could not conceive of its existence without the Levitical offerings. Life was built around this central and controlling practice, and all the while it was pointing, pointing, pointing to the one great event that was to come. God's Lamb would be slain. The religion of the Old Testament focused on this central event of all history – Calvary. Old Testament shadows were soon to become New Testament reality. The message was one – salvation by substitution. Christ the great sin-bearer would take away the sin of the world.

Well did Isaac Watts eloquently pen these words:

> Not all the blood of beasts
> On Jewish altars slain
> Could give the guilty conscience peace,
> Or wash away the stain.
>
> But Christ the heavenly Lamb
> Takes all our sins away;
> A sacrifice of nobler name
> And richer blood than they.
>
> My faith would lay her hand
> On that dear head of Thine,
> While like a penitent I stand
> And there confess my sin.

My soul looks back to see
The burden Thou didst bear,
While hanging on the accursed tree,
And knows her guilt was there.

The Scripture speaks of 'the bringing in of a better hope, through which we draw near to God' (Heb. 7:19).

3. In The Feasts (Leviticus 23)
God instituted the feasts which became an integral part of Israeli society. There were seven main feasts. The Passover, the Feast of Unleavened Bread, the Feast of First-fruits and the Feast of Weeks or Pentecost, followed each other closely. Then there was an interval of four months. In the seventh month, there was the Feast of Trumpets, the Day of Atonement and the Feast of Tabernacles. Three times a year all the males of Israel were to appear before the Lord their God: at the Passover, the Feast of Weeks or Pentecost and the Feast of Tabernacles (Ex. 23:14-17).

The Passover was instituted when the Israelites were slaves in Egypt. Because of the shed blood they were 'passed over' by the angel of death (Ex. 12:13). The lamb died that they might live. The blood was the foundation of everything. It was the beginning of a new and separate nation. With the Christian it is the same, for when his sins are cleansed by Christ's blood it is a new beginning, a new life.

83

It was Jehovah's feast; a feast in anticipation of the death of Christ! The Lord Jesus fulfilled the type in every detail. The great work was accomplished and multitudes could now hear, believe and rejoice in God's great salvation.

The Feast of Unleavened Bread. This began the day after the Passover and continued for seven days. It points to the whole course and character of the believer's life. Feeding on the Bread of life is the believer's sustenance, and the exclusion of leaven speaks of holiness of heart and life, for leaven is a type of sin. To feed on Him is strength and purity.

The Feast of First-Fruits. Whilst the feast of unleavened bread was still in progress this third feast took place. The wilderness was not their dwelling-place. God brought them to 'a land of wheat and barley, of vines and fig trees and pomegranates' (Deut. 8:7-9). In the midst of this wonderful prosperity in Canaan they were to remember the Lord who brought them there. They offered the sheaf of the first-fruits as they reaped the harvest year after year, and in addition offered a lamb on that day as well.

This all foreshadowed another Lamb, another First-fruit, another harvest. Jesus was the slain Lamb, and He rose first from the dead. He was the First-fruit. Israel has failed to acknowledge Him and for this reason Israel's harvests of blessing lie still unreaped, and the great Husbandman has gone forth to other fields which are 'already white for harvest' (John 4:35). There can be no doubt but that the resurrection is in view. Paul says, 'Christ the firstfruits, afterward those who are Christ's at His coming' (1 Cor. 15:23). He is 'the firstborn from the dead' (Col. 1:18), 'the firstborn among many brethren' (Rom. 8:29). We, together with so many, wave our sheaves with rejoicing in the great ingathering.

Pentecost, or the Feast of Weeks. Fifty days after the wave-sheaf had been presented, Pentecost was celebrated. Two loaves of bread were offered and waved before the Lord, similar to the sheaf offering. The loaves were made of the same grain reaped from the same field, so with the descent of the Spirit at Pentecost we are made to be one with Him who was raised from the dead. We become 'the church of the First-born' (Heb. 12:23). The indwelling Spirit seals our oneness with Christ. We are 'the first-fruits of the Spirit' (Rom. 8:23). The presence of Christ in us unites us to God and to each other.

A long period of four months intervened between Pentecost and the Feast of Trumpets. This represents the period of this present age.

The Feast of Trumpets. This begins the second series of Jehovah's feasts. It will have its grand fulfilment in that day when 'the Lord Himself will descend from heaven with a shout, with the voice of an archangel, and with the trumpet of God' (1 Thess. 4:16).

85

The Day of Atonement (Lev. 16). The Day of Atonement was Israel's annual cleansing from sin. Two goats were chosen. The sins of the people were confessed on the head of the one, and it was then led out into the wilderness to die, signifying that their sins were taken into a land of forgetfulness. The other goat was killed and the High Priest went into the Holy of Holies sprinkling its blood on the mercy-seat as an atonement for the nation. This was done only once a year. On no other occasion did the High Priest enter the Holy of Holies. Clearly this points to the one offering of Jesus Christ, God's Lamb who 'entered in once into the holy place, having obtained eternal redemption for us' (Heb. 9:12). The whole event is fully explained and applied in Hebrews chapter 9.

The Feast of Tabernacles. This was a season of great joy at the completion of the harvest, the final fulfilment of the antitype is still in the future. The feast lasted eight days when they lived in booths made of tree branches, reminding them of the days when God cared for them as a nation in the wilderness.

It is obvious that the life of the early Israelite was dominated by the consciousness of God. Offerings had to be sacrificed and journeys were constantly made to attend the feasts. Their lives were religious and all this religion was prophetic in essence and practice. It all pointed forward to a far greater fulfilment than the actual execution of all the religious duties.

The New Testament assumes the history and religious practices of the Old Testament. If there was no Old Testament, hundreds of passages in the New Testament would be utterly meaningless. If the Old Testament is not God's Word, the whole assumption and attitude of the New Testament is completely misguided and wrong. The New Testament bears witness that the Old Testament is of divine origin. In fact if the Old Testament is not the Word of God, the New Testament, which bases its teaching upon the Old Testament, cannot be either. The Old Testament is the very warp and woof of the New Testament, and there are hundreds of allusions affirming its message and establishing its fulfilment. If the Old Testament is not the Word of God, Christ was wrong, the apostles were wrong and we have all been led astray. But Christ, by His life and actions fulfilled the very heart and nature, the intricacies and details of Old Testament predictions, pictures and illustrations. The church, by its very existence, endorses the foreshadowings of the world-wide spread of gospel truths. We can but stand back in the face of such overwhelming evidence and declare with full assurance that the documents of the Old and New Testaments have the stamp of divinity and can be nothing other than the Word of God.

Chapter 5

ITS ARCHAEOLOGY

Biblical archaeology is a fascinating science which unravels the past and authenticates the history of the written records. It provides a general background of biblical history, fills out biblical stories, helps us to understand difficult passages and confirms the value and truth of the Old Testament record. In doing so it deals a fatal blow to those radical critical theories which have plagued, in particular, Old Testament study. Before archaeological research, reams of sheer nonsense were written by scholars who regarded the Bible as myth and unreliable legend. Acting as a corrective and a purge, archaeology has eliminated many erratic theories and false assumptions.

Nearly all important archaeological discoveries are comparatively modern and these have shed a brilliant light upon the Old Testament world making it one of the freshest and most fascinating studies of the day. Only in the last 150 years has this subject opened up. In fact, in the first half of the nineteenth century, Greek and Egyptian history went back only to 650 BC, and everything before that was labelled as prehistoric myth. Now however, we can go back far beyond that date and make statements about life in those far off days with absolute certainty.

Hundreds of thousands of cuneiform tablets and documents have been uncovered and our knowledge of Old Testament times has increased immeasurably. The biblical narrative (at any rate from Abraham onwards) falls well within attested history. It is interesting to note that no archaeological evidence has disproved the Scriptures.

Merrill Unger points out that archaeology authenticates the Bible. It illustrates, explains and supplements the Bible.

Ability to Write

The question of writing was a thorny issue. Was Moses able to write? This was dismissed as altogether impossible and therefore the Pentateuch was regarded as myth recorded by a number of later writers. However, an alphabetical inscription was found on a stone at Byblos which goes back to 1250 BC. The writings found at Lachish go back a further fifty years. At Bethshemesh an inscription in Phoenician is ascribed to 1400 BC. A discovery in Sinai shows that Syrian workmen were familiar with the art of writing in 1500 BC. The laws of Hammurabi, king of Babylon (1792-1750 BC), were discovered at Susa in 1902 on a stele containing 282 laws. The code of Eshnunna, an ancient city north-east of Baghdad predates the Code of Hammurabi by two centuries. It was finally conceded that Moses, who probably crossed the Red Sea in 1441 BC, could write! In fact he could have written in Egyptian hieroglyphics for 'Moses was learned in all the wisdom of the Egyptians' (Acts 7:22), or in Akkadian, as the Amarna letters of the fourteenth century BC show, or in ancient Hebrew, as the discovery in 1929-31 of the Ugaritic literature at Ras Shamra in North Syria demonstrates.[1]

Patriarchal Period

The biblical account of the patriarchal age is now considered to reflect with remarkable accuracy the actual conditions of the period. Abraham emerges from the dim and misty past where his adventures were thought to be mythical or legendary, with vivid clarity and historical precision.

Opinions differ as to the exact date for the Patriarchs, but archaeologists generally place them between 1900 and 1700 BC. More than one hundred thousand inscribed clay tablets dated to this period have been found.[2] Numerous parallels between these excavated writings and the biblical accounts have been demonstrated, and the figure of Abraham fits exactly into the world of that day.

It was customary for childless couples of that day to adopt a boy who would yield all his rights to the real heir on the birth of a son. Abraham chose Eliezer but Isaac superseded him.

When Sarah gave Hagar to Abraham to provide him with children she was but conforming to the practice of that time.[3]

In Joshua 24:2 we read that 'your fathers, *including* Terah, the father of Abraham and the father of Nahor, dwelt on the other side of the River

[River Euphrates] in old times; and they served other gods'. Until 1854, the site of Ur was completely unknown, but today is one of the best known ancient sites of southern Babylonia. It was one of the largest and wealthiest cities of that time. It had a complex system of government and a well developed system of commerce, one with writing in common use for the issue of receipts, the making of contracts and many other purposes.[4]

The great ziggurat, a mountain of brickwork, was erected there. Whilst numerous gods were worshipped in Babylonia, the shrine to the moon god, Nannar, on the ziggurat, was supreme. A whole quarter of the city was set apart for him. He was called the 'Exalted Lord', and similar titles. Upon this great ziggurat Abraham gazed constantly. Many shrines of lesser gods were erected but Nannar was king as well as god and numerous priests and civil servants were in his service. The cult, in Abraham's day, was absolutely inseparable from the city.[5] All that has been unearthed has vindicated the statement that Abraham's family 'served other gods', and the Scripture is substantiated.

It was common practice for a man to become a servant on the condition that his master provided him with a wife as agreed by contract. So Jacob worked for his brides among the Aramean tribe of Laban.[6]

Esau's sale of his birthright has a number of parallels.

Rachel stole her father Laban's gods (Gen.

31:34). Today, because of the Nuzu (or Nuzi) evidence, we know that possession of the household gods implied leadership of the family and the right to the father's property. Rachel's theft therefore was a serious offence, aimed at preserving for her husband her father's estate. Laban evidently had sons of his own and this resulted in his anxiety to retrieve the gods.[7]

There was peculiar significance attached to the words of a dying father in Nuzi. These were held as binding on his sons after his death. This throws light on the importance of some of the last words of the patriarchs (Gen. 27, 49).[8]

The great service of archaeological research in this period is that it demonstrates that the picture of the patriarchs as presented in Genesis fits the frame of contemporary life completely. Thomson states that it is particularly noticeable that a great many of these customs were not known in later times, say in the tenth or ninth century BC. It would have been impossible for Israelites of these later centuries to have had access to such information as we now have, and to have produced the comprehensive picture which is before us. The patriarchal history was not made up of artificial stories composed in the days of the kings. It is clear that we are dealing with a genuine society in the early part of the second millennium BC. Archaeology gives us a solid historical base and compels a respect for the patriarchal stories, for the knowledge of their age has been and is further being recovered from historical evidence. W. F. Albright says: 'Genesis reflects with remarkable accuracy the conditions of ... the period between 1800 and 1500 BC.'[9]

Egypt
Excavations in Egypt have uncovered the same endorsement of the biblical descriptions of the time of Joseph. Egyptian artists depict the investiture of a ruler, and this corresponds exactly to the biblical narrative in which Pharaoh honours Joseph (Gen. 41:42, 43).

The building operations in Egypt are clearly recorded in word and picture and correspond to the biblical records where slaves made bricks and built under the direction of the taskmaster.

Perhaps the most unanswerable bit of testimony that Israel resided in Egypt for a long time is the surprising number of Egyptian names in the Levitical genealogies. For example: Moses, Assir, Pashhur, Hophni, Phinehas and Merari, are all unquestionably Egyptian.[10]

Tel El Amarna on the upper Nile was excavated in 1887 and the thousands of clay tablets which were discovered switched on, as it were, a blazing light on the period of 1380-1320 BC. A vivid picture of the Egyptian empire has been disclosed. In these letters we have the first mention of Uru-salem (Jerusalem) outside of the Old Testament.

Joshua's Conquest

A letter from Jerusalem's king tells of the new enemy called Habiru who are capturing and destroying the land. 'The land is lost to the Habiru.' 'The Habiru have wasted all the territory.'[11] These striking accounts are now generally accepted as the records of the Hebrew invasion of Canaan.

Archaeological evidence is interesting in the conquest of the land. In the south, towns such as Jericho, Lachish, Debir, Eglon and Libnah were taken and destroyed. Work has been done in all of these and it would seem that there was considerable destruction in these towns in about 1250 BC. This fits in well with Joshua's campaign. Other towns, two in particular, Megiddo and Bethshan, seem to have been in Egyptian and Canaanite hands till some time after 1200 BC. Only after some years did the typical Israelite culture, shown by pottery, appear in these towns. This all indicates that while there was a sudden violent conquest at first, pockets of resistance remained and only slowly was the land completely controlled. 'There remaineth yet very much land to be possessed' (Josh. 13:1). The Bible rightly represents the conquest of the land by Israel as being incomplete at the time of Joshua.[12]

Hazor, the mightiest of the Canaanite towns, was protected by great ramparts, but in Joshua 11, we read that Joshua took it and destroyed it by fire. Numerous archaeological reports from respected archaeologists show that Hazor was indeed destroyed by fire at the time when the Israelites

95

invaded the country. Archaeologists have been compelled to identify the destruction of Hazor with the Israelite conquest. The four-foot layer of ash-filled earth shows that a destructive conflagration took place at that time.

Bethel was another of the sites referred to as being conquered by Joshua (Josh. 8). The town was destroyed by a mighty conflagration leaving a deposit of as much as over a metre of debris. Albright and others acknowledge this to be the work of the invading Israelites.

At every turn the archaeologist's spade endorses, supplements, clarifies and vindicates the biblical record.

The Period of the Kings

The principal building at Gibeah, from Saul's era, had massive stone constructions and deep walls. Albright says, 'Saul was only a rustic chieftain, as far as architecture and amenities of life were concerned.'[13] This accords with the biblical record.

Modern critics tended to deny or drastically minimise David's activity in organising Hebrew sacred music. Now, however, archaeology has illuminated the subject to such an extent to show that there is nothing incongruous in the light of conditions in 1000 BC. There is incontrovertible evidence for the existence of musical guilds. The Canaanites especially were able musicians and Hebrew music probably went back to pre-Israelite sources. Again the critics have been silenced by the evidence of the archaeologist's spade.[14]

The vast achievements of Solomon are well researched. He built up a considerable force of chariots for the army, concentrating them in chariot cities. In 1928, Megiddo yielded the evidence of a chariot city where at least 450 horses and 150 chariots were kept. Solomon's stables are part of today's tourist attractions at Megiddo. The Bible said that 'Solomon had horses imported from Egypt' (1 Kings 10:28), and now that statement is abundantly proved not only by the excavations at Megiddo, but also by those at Taanach and Tel el Hesi in the south.[15] Jerusalem, Hazor, Megiddo and Gezer are mentioned as chariot cities (1 Kings 9:15-19, 10:26).

Solomon's great activity in smelting and working of metals was confirmed by the excavation, in 1938-40, of the flourishing town of Ezion Geber on the Red Sea. These were quite clearly worked in the days of Solomon. The amazing furnaces and ancient crucibles were uncovered. The refining process was carried out in a highly technical manner using the strong north winds to heat the furnaces. It was here, at Ezion Geber, that Solomon made a navy of ships and from here conducted considerable commercial trade (1 Kings 9:26-28).[16] The biblical accounts are all supported by the revelations of the excavations. The discovery of the copper refinery at Tel el Kheleifeh illustrates the important biblical reference to copper smelting and casting in the Jordan valley (1 Kings 7:46), and points to another source of Solomon's wealth.

The excavations of Solomon's temple indicate that he drew heavily upon Phoenician skill and technology, and this we find recorded in 1 Kings 5:18 and in 1 Kings 7:13-14. Similar ground plans of sanctuaries of the general period 1200-900 BC have been excavated in North Syria and the findings have demonstrated that the specifications of the Solomonic structure in 1 Kings 6 and 7 are pre-Greek and authentic for the tenth century BC. The temple is not to be assigned to the period of Hellenistic influence after the sixth century BC as some critics were accustomed to do.[17] We now know of temples in Syria of the same period as that of Solomon which are also divided into three parts. Aerial photographs can also be studied, and these facts affirmed.[18] The archaeologists have done great service to those who believe the truth of God's Word, and they have again silenced the critics.

When Solomon died, Jeroboam appealed to Shishak of Egypt for help to quell tribal factions. Shishak invaded Judah and sacked Jerusalem (1 Kings 14:25, 26; 2 Chron. 12:2-4), continuing on his conquering northbound campaign. One of his inscribed stelae was found at Megiddo, telling of his deeds. This together with the inscription on the wall of the temple at Karnak confirms the biblical records.

Although the Bible speaks of Omri, king of Israel (876-869 BC) in only six verses (1 Kings 16:23-28), he established Samaria and with him began a new era of Israelite power. His son Ahab (869-850 BC) continued the successful policies of his father and developed Samaria as a royal city of power and influence. The Monolith Inscription, now in the British Museum, records the advance of the mighty Assyrians and mentions amongst their enemies, 'Ahab the Israelite'.[19]

In Isaiah 20:1, we have an obscure reference to 'Sargon, the king of Assyria'. Before archaeological investigations, this was the only mention of this enigmatic figure, and it was therefore dismissed as worthless. The Bible's record was regarded as of no consequence. But in 1943 Sargon's palace was discovered at Khorsabad, and further investigations have since been made. With the recovery of the palace, the royal annals and other records of Sargon's reign (722-705 BC), he is now one of the best known of the Assyrian monarchs, particularly as the king who conquered Samaria after the three-year siege by Shalmaneser V.[20] So the Bible was accurate after all!

In 2 Kings 18 and 19, we have the story of Sennacherib's mighty Assyrian army sweeping victoriously through Judah, conquering its cities and laying siege to Jerusalem. God sent the angel of death to the Assyrian camp and 185,000 men were killed. The Assyrians retreated and Hezekiah and the city were saved. The Assyrians' version of this war is recorded on the Taylor Prism in the British Museum: 'As for Hezekiah the Jew, who did not submit to my yoke, forty-six of his strong walled cities, as well as the small cities in their neighbourhood ... I besieged and took ... Himself, like a caged bird, I shut up in Jerusalem his royal city.' There is no mention of the hasty conclusion of his Palestinian campaign and his sudden withdrawal to Nineveh! The biblical story is completely vindicated as well as being embellished by the graphic descriptions of the Assyrians. It is significant that nowhere does Sennacherib actually claim to have taken Jerusalem. His account fills out the biblical narrative with lively details and once again gives us confidence in the biblical story.

In 2 Kings 20:20, we read that Hezekiah 'made a pool, and a conduit, and brought water into the city'. The great conduit, or tunnel, of Hezekiah, 1777 feet long and hewn out of solid rock is an amazing achievement. At the end of the tunnel Hezekiah constructed a pool called the Pool of Siloam. To accomplish this task men dug from both sides, meeting in the middle, and in the tunnel they left an inscription commemorating the completion of the work. We do not need to go to any library to assess the truth of the biblical statement today for we can simply walk through it and experience with wonder and awe (and cold, wet feet!) Hezekiah's great achievement, affirming once again that the Scriptural statements are true.

The case of Belshazzar, the last king of Babylon is another issue where the Bible has been proved correct. Because the Bible makes Belshazzar king at the time of the fall of Babylon (Daniel 5), instead of Nabonidus, as the cuneiform records show, the biblical record was thought to be void of truth. Later, however, when further evidence was uncovered it was found that Nabonidus spent the last part of his reign in Arabia and left the conduct of the kingdom to his eldest son Belshazzar.[21] Once again the biblical record is proved to be true.

One striking example of prophecy is the predicted fate of the ancient city of Tyre described in Ezekiel 26:3-14. Note the order of events. Many nations were to come against Tyre like the waves of the sea (verse 3). The first of these was to be led by Nebuchadnezzar, King of Babylon. History records that it was only after a siege of 13 years that Nebuchadnezzar finally took the city. The Tyrians removed to an island half a mile from the shore and left the ancient city desolate. Verses 4 and 5 and 12-14, however, remained unfulfilled, which stated that the ruins were to be broken down and placed 'in the midst of the sea'. The towers of the ancient city remained and these words awaited 240 years for their fulfilment. Then Alexander the Great determined to capture the island city of Tyre by land and built a causeway through the waters. In order to do so he broke down the walls and towers and houses of the old city and, as foretold, 'lay your stones, your timber, and your soil in the midst of the water' (verse 12). Ancient Tyre is literally today like 'the top of a rock', a place 'for the spreading of nets'. Its desolation is complete. In his great work, 'The Land and the Book', Thompson, the writer, referring to the causeway made in the sea of which parts still remain today, says: 'The number of granite columns that lie in the sea, particularly on the north of the island, is surprising. The east wall of the inner harbour is entirely founded upon them, and they are thickly spread over the bottom of the sea on every side.'[22]

Light is shed on a number of small incidents. For instance, the Bible states that the people of Israel smote the enemy 'with the edge of the sword' (Ex. 17:13, Num. 21:24, etc.). In Hebrew, the phrase is literally 'to the mouth of the sword'. This turns out to be a precise description. Many of the swords, daggers and battle-axes which have been excavated have the representation of an animal mouth at the top of the blade so that the blade appears to issue from the jaws of the wild beasts. The phrase 'to devour to the mouth of the sword' is a very vivid one indeed.[23]

At the beginning of this century peasants in Elephantine near to the Aswan Dam on the Nile, discovered hundreds of ancient papyri. They were written in the Jewish language and dated between the years 494 and 400 BC, covering the period just before and after Nehemiah. The keeping of the Passover is mentioned as well as names such as 'King Darius II', and 'Sanballat, Governor of Samaria'.[24]

The New Testament Period

The discovery in the last 150 years of manuscripts and versions has given valuable aid to the whole field of textual research. The true meaning and literary nature of words and phrases, pronunciation and syntax (i.e., the relation of one word to another in the sentence) of the Greek in the New Testament has been greatly advanced.

New Testament scholarship has often been plagued with extremism but archaeological research has brought balance and a more accurate understanding to the whole scene.

John's Gospel was placed as late as the second half of the second century, removing it from authentic apostolic tradition. A small papyrus fragment containing John 18:31-33, 37, 38, was published in 1935, and is now in the John Rylands Library in Manchester. It is the oldest known fragment of the New Testament. It is competently dated within the period 100-150 AD which immediately destroys the late second-century hypothesis. In addition, the Qumran documents of the Dead Sea Scrolls since 1947, show that the supposed second-century Gnostic ideas of John's gospel are authentic to first century Jewish life and thought, and substantiate the traditional first-century date of John's gospel, placing it within the apostolic period.[25] Archaeology has rescued John's gospel from relegation to the file of non-genuine and non-authentic documents.

Claims were often made that Christianity was

strongly influenced by the mystery religions of the East. However, discoveries in Palestine, Syria and Egypt have eliminated these notions. Excavations have uncovered no documents or buildings belonging to such sects. Heathen temples, Jewish synagogues and Christian churches have been found, but a conspicuous absence of other religious structures prevails. The Christian faith emerges as a unique historical phenomenon like the faith of Israel that preceded it. Archaeology proves Christianity to be unspoilt by the religions and philosophies of the day.[26]

A great mass of documents has come to light in the vernacular Greek, illustrating and illuminating the cultural and social conditions of the New Testament world. In 1945, a whole library of Gnostic literature was discovered in Upper Egypt, pouring light on their doctrines and illustrating how dangerous they were. To attempt to identify Gnostic tenets with the teaching of Jesus and especially that of John, is now seen to be totally untenable.[27] In fact, warnings against the Gnostics in the New Testament writings are now clearly evident because their teachings have been exposed by archaeology and the apostles' cautions recognized.

At Delphi, an inscription has been found making it possible to date the arrival of the proconsul Gallio at Corinth in the summer of AD 51, and to conclude that Paul came to the city at the beginning of AD 50. This enables the whole of the Pauline itinerary to be dated and is a valuable point of reference, for

Paul appeared before him eighteen months after coming to the city (Acts 18:11-17).[28]

Excavations at Corinth, Athens, Philippi, Ephesus and other sites evangelized by Paul, make these towns much better known, showing that the Scriptural stories fit precisely.

Archaeology illustrates from the Roman invasion in AD 70, which was predicted by Christ, the thoroughness of the interruption, not only of Jewish communal life in Palestine, but that of Christianity as well. Not a single synagogue of the early Roman period survived, nor did normal community life resume in Jerusalem after its destruction, for no Jewish tombs in the region of Jerusalem can be dated after AD 70. All inscribed ossuaries (i.e., the stone receptacles for the bones of the dead), in this region belong to the period 30-70 AD.[29] The Roman invasion was a terrible blow to the Jewish nation scattering it far and wide. This is attested by archaeology.

The Acts of the Apostles is now accepted as the work of a very careful historian. So many historical and geographical details have been uncovered that the theories which existed to discredit Luke's writings have been rendered futile.

Luke clearly implied, for instance, in Acts 14:6, that Iconium was in Phrygia, while Derbe and Lystra were 'cities of Lycaonia'. Pliny agreed with Luke, but other early writers including Cicero, assigned it to Lycaonia. Criticism against Luke's accuracy resulted. In 1910, however, an inscribed monument was discovered which demonstrated that Iconium was a thoroughly Phrygian city and the Phrygian tongue was still employed as late as the middle of the third century AD. Numbers of other inscriptions substantiate the fact that the city could be described as Phrygian and administratively as Galatian. Confidence in Luke's accuracy was restored.[30]

Another difficulty was Luke's use of the Greek word *meris* to mean a geographical 'region' or 'district' when describing Philippi (Acts 16:12). Many thought that Luke had blundered badly until excavations in the papyri-rich sands of the Fayum in Egypt demonstrated that many who had emigrated from Macedonia, where Philippi was located, used that very word to denote the divisions of a district. Now all scholars own that Luke used the word correctly, and archaeology has again furnished evidence to vindicate Luke's impeccable accuracy.[31]

At Thessalonica, Luke used the term 'politarchs' for the leaders who headed the people's assembly (Acts 17:5-9). This title occurred nowhere else in Greek literature, and Luke's reliability was seriously questioned. Further excavations in this area have produced at least seventeen inscriptions using this term, and Luke's accuracy is once again vindicated.[32]

The biblical picture of Herod is altogether in agreement with his character as known from extra-biblical sources. In Matthew 2:1-23, we read of his insane jealousy and suspicion. At the very mention by the Magi, of a rival claimant to the throne, 'Where is that is born king of the Jews?' (Matt. 2:2), his murderous plots were set in motion. He not only brutally murdered the children in the Bethlehem area, but his murders included numerous members of his own family, including his favourite wife, Mariamne and her sons. Caesar Augustus was said to have exclaimed, 'I would rather be Herod's hog than his son.'[33] Again archaeology has confirmed the accurate biblical assessment of his character and crimes.

Tacitus mentions the fact that Christ was put to death under Tiberius by the procurator Pontius Pilate, so the Scriptural event is confirmed by extra-biblical history.

The magnificent building activities of Herod the Great are evident. He expanded Jerusalem considerably. His most elaborate project was the temple, which was begun in 20-19 BC. The Pharisees declared that the temple in Jesus' day had been in the process of construction for forty-six years (John 2:20), which accords with the archaeological evidence. He built a superb wall with its gates, around the great court in which the temple stood. There was Solomon's Porch, where Jesus taught (John 10:23) and where Peter and the apostles later preached (Acts 3:11; 5:12). There was the Sheep Gate (John 5:2), and the Beautiful Gate where the lame beggar was daily laid (Acts 3:2). All these are verified by the excavations.

Discovered coins are numerous, and they

confirm over and over the times of the Caesars and the various rulers. These are significant confirmations of biblical remarks concerning these men and their periods of rulership.

A beautiful picture has been unearthed of men carrying the seven-branched candlestick as booty in the triumphal procession after the fall of Jerusalem in 70 AD. It was therefore not merely a prophecy of Jesus, it actually happened historically.

Confirmation of Paul's free Roman status is found in the history of Tarsus. When Rome took over in 64 BC, Tarsus became the seat of the governmental administration of the province of Cilicia. Unger states:

> 'It was probably when Antony decreed full Roman citizenship on all the Tarsians (including the Jews), that Saul's family received the important benefit, which stood the apostle in good stead when later this fact changed the attitude of Roman governmental officialdom toward him and gave him the right to appeal to Caesar (Acts 22:28-30). These privileges were confirmed by Augustus, so that Tarsus became a favoured town and its citizens proud of its civic-mindedness and progress.'[34]

Paul could gladly say, 'I am a Jew from Tarsus, in Cilicia, a citizen of no mean city' (Acts 21:39).

Ephesus has been a rich source of archaeological discovery. In particular, the fabulous temple of Artemis (Diana) is seen to be of immense proportions and of magnificent character. Many statuettes of the goddess have been uncovered. It all illustrates Paul's activities and conflict in this strategic, bustling, wealthy metropolis with its splendid harbour and fertile valley stretching into the interior of Asia Minor (Acts 19).

It is now perfectly understandable why Paul chose to spend two years in this important mission field with the result that 'all who dwelt in Asia heard the word of the Lord Jesus, both Jews and Greeks' (Acts 19:10). The apostle's success in Ephesus was so great that the mighty temple of Artemis and its devotees were seriously affected (Acts 19). It is entirely understandable that the manufacturers of the small shrines of Diana and of the goddess herself would riot and yell for two hours, 'Great *is* Diana of the Ephesians!' (Acts 19:28).

Archaeology has illustrated, clarified, supplemented and authenticated the New Testament record. Its unanswerable evidence makes the Scriptures better understood and more widely accepted by all, even by those scholars who only recognize pure science and place little or no value on the belief that the Bible is the Word of God.

Archaeology cannot actually prove the Bible to be the Word of God but it establishes the biblical record as genuine, dismissing criticisms and foolish arguments with factual contempt and rejoicing the hearts of those who believe in its inerrancy and trust in its divine authorship. It undergirds the biblical message and establishes confidence in even its smallest details.

Dig on, dig on, O archaeologists! We have nothing to fear. Your evidence will but corroborate and establish the truth that the Bible is the very Word of God.

Chapter 6

ITS SUPERIORITY

It is not necessary to depreciate the literature of other religions in order to exalt the Bible. There is wisdom, truth, beauty and spiritual thought in the books of non-Christian faiths. They are associated with various civilizations of the world. But do any of them possess the qualities which would fit them to be the supreme literature guide of the world? Does any one of them rise above all others, or must we find the Bible to be so far in advance of these books that it is instinctively recognized as being vastly superior and in every way fitted to lead men to God and to moral living? Let us consider the writings of some of the major religions of the world.

Buddhism

Buddhism was begun in the sixth century BC. It has a vast variety of doctrine and practice and is really an evolutionary process to be achieved by one's own effort, addressing itself primarily to the problem of pain and suffering rather than that of moral evil. It has been described as 'a non-theistic ethical discipline'. In Buddhism we have an agnosticism which cannot find personal religion. The books of such a mode of living must fall short of the conditions by which they alone could claim to supersede all others.

111

Buddhism has often become embedded in culture and is on many occasions more a way of life than a religion, for it has no place for a god or gods. Its earliest documents date from the seventh century AD. It fails completely to convince men of sin and to offer a Saviour from that sinful state. It fails completely to lead men to God.

Confucianism

'The sacred books of China bring us face to face with the practical paradox, that, while none have ever been more influential in moulding the life of a people, no inspiration or supernatural authority is claimed for them.... Their guardians are not so much priests as scholars. The five chief books of Confucianism ... are partly the original work of the master, partly compilations and selections by him from pre-existing literature, with possibly, to some small extent, later editions.... Its fundamental lesson is the inculcation of reverence, and it is full of finely conceived and inspiring thoughts.'[1]

Confucianism has much of an ethical quality and moral purpose, but Confucius (551-497 BC) did not formulate a system of thought. He did not contribute any new idea to that which was there, but the body of his writings perpetuated the existing system. Confucian philosophy was influenced by and influenced Buddhism. It is distinguished by its ethical rather than its religious teaching. Confucius taught that inner goodness finds expression in outward behaviour. He was unusual in that he was both founder and author. 'In general, the Confucian ethical ideal is simply for every person to do his proper part in the immediate relationships of life.'[2] In these writings Hastings states: 'there is a determined adherence to the level of the purely human, an avoidance of all reference to the divine.'[3] The teaching consists of four main features, providence, secondary spirits, ancestral worship and the imperial sacrifice when the Emperor offered a calf in sacrifice, not in expiation but in homage to the Supreme Ruler of all.

While Confucianism has refining and beautiful thoughts it fails to direct the soul to a personal God. There is no vital and intimate encounter or communion with a living, loving Saviour. Whilst all men recognize wrong and evil, Confucianism provides no answer to the problem. What must be done with my sin? How can I come into contact with Almighty God? These questions, which are at the heart of man's needs, are left unanswered by a system which has no atoning sacrifice, no forgiveness, no assurance of salvation or of God's presence either now or in the future.

Hinduism
Hinduism, dating from about 1500 BC, consists of a welter of beliefs and practices. The genius for syncretism has been the strength of Hinduism. It is an extremely idolatrous and polytheistic religion with millions of gods. There are numerous contradictions in the Hindu scriptures, with a great

deal of variation in its many teachings. It has absorbed innumerable customs and concepts which have produced many schools of Hindu thought. No authority can be applied for there is no final word of scripture which would be applicable to all its factions. 'Indians are immersed in folklore and legends about the exploits of the various gods and goddesses.... There are many books and they often contradict one another.'[4] Hindus would disagree amongst themselves as to the value and authority of their own writings.

Strange scientific inaccuracies are to be found such as the moon shining with its own light, and the earth being flat and being borne on the heads of numerous elephants.

In all these Hindu writings we find a total absence of a real solution to the problem of sin and misery, of a standard of absolute righteousness, of deliverance from sin and of a blessed and eternal state in the presence of God.

Shintoism

Shintoism, the indigenous religion of Japan, has been influenced by Buddhism, Confucianism, and more recently, Christianity. Kenneth Boa says: 'It is a combination of many things, and within it are wide differences of thought and practice.... It centres on the worship of nature deities and deified people. It has no founder, no prophet, no saviour, and little formal doctrine.'[5] Its two main books were produced in 712 and 720 AD. 'Unlike the Bible,

Shinto is based on nebulous stories devoid of any historical facts.' The two eighth century books 'are entirely unverifiable.'[6] Stories reminiscent of Greek mythology abound. Nature deities such as the gods of wind, sun, sea, trees and fire exist in the Shinto pantheon. These writings surely cannot merit universal acclaim.

Islam

Mohammed received visions for twenty-two years before his death in 632 AD, and these he recited to his followers who wrote them down. This eventually became the Qur'an (Koran), the sacred book of the Muslims. It combines elements from Judaism and Christianity and accepts Noah, Abraham, Moses, David, Jesus, John and others as prophets of Allah. It is a little shorter than the New Testament. All the sects within Islam use the Koran which teaches a strict monotheism and denounces all forms of idol worship. It is the authoritative scripture of Islam divided into 114 surahs (chapters). Muslims believe that all earlier forms of revelation are in corrupted form and the Koran supersedes them. Whenever there is a conflict between the Koran and the Bible, Muslims say that the Bible is not accurate and has been changed by men, whereas the Koran is eternal. Muslims have a distorted picture of the Trinity and think that it consists of three Gods. This to them is totally unacceptable. They reject the crucifixion of Jesus Christ. A. C. Bouquet states:

'Very little is taught but what can be deduced from passages in the Old Testament or some of the apocalyptic literature.... The matter is for the most part borrowed but the manner is all the prophet's own. Firsthand knowledge of the Bible is scanty and comes late, but there are frequent evidences of dependence upon Rabbinic legends, and upon Christian traditions from distorted apocryphal sources.... The canonical gospels themselves do not seem to have been studied.'[7]

'Mohammed, writing in the Koran, refers to the Old and New Testaments as the truth, but his doctrines often contradict their teachings.'[8]

'In his book *Islam and Christianity*, J. W. Sweetman gives much evidence of Mohammed's dependence on human sources for the Koran, and that its claim to be pure Arabic is not founded on fact.'[9] Words used are derived from a variety of sources in both Jewish and Aramaic writings and from other documents as well. Jeffrey in 'Foreign Vocabulary of the Koran', 'has gathered some 300 pages dealing with foreign words in the Koran ... which refutes Mohammed's claim that the Koran is pure Arabic.'[10] In the Koran's rigid predestination of all human actions it has within itself a moral code, 'but this code is immeasurably lower in its standard than that of Christ and His gospel – which absolutely disproves the claims of Mohammed that the Koran is "Final Revelation!"'[11] says Copleston.

Islam certainly does not emphasize the problem of sin and has very little consciousness of it. In contrast to Christianity which calls for inward holiness not outward form, Islam proposes self-righteous works as a means of salvation. It is externalistic with no vital personal relationship with God. The five pillars of Islam are:

1. The Recitation of the Creed.
2. Prayer – five times a day.
3. Almsgiving.
4. The month of fasting – Ramadan.
5. Pilgrimage to Mecca.

In addition to these a sixth is often added – the holy War – Jihad. The use of force is sanctioned in the Koran and soldiers who die in such a war to spread Islam are assured of their entry into heaven which is a place of sensuous enjoyment.

Copleston points out that there are a number of absurdities in the Koran. Allah commands Satan to worship Adam (Sura 15:28-39, 20:114, 115 etc.). In this instance therefore Allah joins Adam to him to receive Satan's worship, but in Sura 18:110 and Sura 4:116, he says 'God truly will not forgive the joining of other gods with Himself.'

Allah is seen to be a misleader. In Sura 6:39, we read: 'God will mislead whom he pleases.' In several other suras we find this same concept (e.g. Suras 7:176 and 7:185). In Sura 28:14, Satan is declared to be a misleader. So both Satan and Allah are misleaders!

In Sura 51:57, we read: 'I have not created jinn and men but that they should worship me.' In Sura

117

7:176, however, we read: 'Moreover many of the jinn and men we have created for Hell.' This is a direct contradiction.

Despite the declaration that there is to be no compulsion in religion, and Mohammed is only a warner, in grossest contradiction we have commands to destroy the infidels. In Sura 2:258, we read, 'Let there be no compulsion in religion', and in Sura 22:48, we read, 'Say O man! I am only a warner'. But in Sura 47:4, we read, 'When ye encounter infidels, strike off their heads till ye have made a great slaughter among them'. Mohammed commands his disciples to kill those who oppose his claims. Christ commands His disciples to bless those who curse them and to do good to those who hate them (Matt. 5:43, 44). 'The absolute contrast of hate and love is sufficient of itself to prove the falsity of Islam.'[12]

The Koran reveals Allah to be so transcendent that he is practically unknowable. Even though he is all-powerful he is arbitrary in his decisions and actions. The Koran makes no provision for sin's forgiveness. There is no certainty of salvation because it is based on a works system. All will be revealed at the day of judgment. It appeals to the motives of fear and reward, and it relies upon the method of force. It is pervaded by a great sense of fatalism. Its heaven is excessively sensuous and carnal. In practice its estimate of woman is low and in Muslim countries women have few rights.

The Koran fails to speak of God's holiness which

requires His punishment for sin, for the life will be weighed and assessed at the judgment. It fails to speak of the expiation of transgression by the sacrifice which God in His great love initiated; of the assurance of pardon for sin; of the marvellous regeneration by the indwelling Spirit of God which transforms men and women and makes them new. The Koran fails to meet man's need and give him communion with the living God.

The Koran is therefore unfitted to become a book of a universal religion. Allah does not enter into humanity and therefore cannot render to humanity the highest service.

The writings of the world's religions in comparison with the Bible, are seen to be unhistorical. Their teachings are not worked out step by step in the life of a people. Their doctrines are announced, explained and circumscribed by comment and ritual, but they have no prophets to apply the words to the circumstances in the nation which would have clarified their meaning.

In addition, ritual and ceremony have overpowered the strivings of the human heart after a personal and spiritual fellowship with God, and externalism has in many cases taken the place of intimate communion. The teachings fail to introduce men to God. Some are religious philosophies, some are nationalistic and some are mythological. Some combine all of these characteristics but all fail to provide proof of the divine quality of their writings.

The Bible

The Bible is supreme in both style and substance, in method and message, in communication and content. It stands in a class by itself.

Its Style

Huxley, the great scientist, says of the Bible that 'it abounds in exquisite beauty of pure literary form.'[13] The Bible has a charming simplicity of language which children can understand, yet it contains the noblest thoughts which grip the minds of the highest intelligence. There is ease of expression, enormous pathos and matchless sublimity. There are homely pictures, noble thoughts, fascinating stories and beautiful expressions. It stimulates the intellect, stirs the emotions and moves the heart. There are many styles of composition – prose, dramatic poetry, lyric poetry, elegy, rhapsody, history, prophecy, vision, allegory, parable, proverb – and yet we find marvellous harmony even in the widest divergence of matter and style.

Robert Lee gives a few literary comments made on books of the Bible as follows:

The book of Ruth. This book is a literary and spiritual gem. The great literary authority of the eighteenth century, Dr. Samuel Johnson, introduced and read it to his friends in a London club, a pastoral which he said he had lately met with and which they imagined had only just been composed; and when they were loud in their praises of its simple and pathetic beauty, he informed them that it was only the story of Ruth which he had read them from a book they all despised – the Bible. There is nothing in human literature more beautiful than Ruth's address to her mother-in-law (1:16, 17) – it is sublime.

The book of Job. Tennyson called it 'the greatest poem whether of ancient or modern literature'. Carlyle wrote: 'I call that (Job) one of the grandest things ever written with pen.'

The book of Jeremiah. Isaac Williams says: 'There is nothing in all Scripture so eloquent of love and sorrow and consolation as the XXXI and XXXIII chapters of Jeremiah. No words can be found in any language of such touching beauty.'

The book of Lamentations. Principal Whyte writes: 'There is nothing like the Lamentations of Jeremiah in the whole world. There has been plenty of sorrow in every age, and in every land, but such another preacher and author, with such a heart for sorrow, has never again been born. Dante comes next to Jeremiah, and we know that Jeremiah was that great exile's favourite prophet.'

The book of Jonah. That eminent literary authority and author, Charles Reade, declared that the book of Jonah is the most beautiful story ever written in so small a compass.

The book of Habakkuk. Viewed simply as literature ... this book stands supreme for its literary beauty. It is said that Benjamin Franklin read Habakkuk to a literary circle in Paris, winning their unanimous tribute of admiration for an author of whom not one of them had ever heard before. Habakkuk's description of the majesty and self-revelations of God in chapter 3 stands supreme.[14]

With regard to the book of Psalms there are numerous tributes to this body of writings which deal with mankind in all aspects of life. Man's existence is chequered by trial, danger and bereavement, and the whole range and sweep of human emotions is laid bare. Man's inmost heart is exposed with, at times, heart-rending grief, and at others passionate longing for divine assistance. Ardent zeal, fervour, passion, trepidation, cordiality, joy, ecstasy – it's all there. It reflects every mood in man's changing scene.

As literature the Bible is superior to all the writings of men and only by the inspiration of God can this come about. God is the author of its beauty and harmony. God is the author of its accuracy and purity. God is the author of its eloquence and nobility. God communicates in sublime simplicity and enchanting cadence, and His Word convinces the intellect, touches the heart, stirs the emotions and activates the will.

Its Content

In His high priestly prayer in John 17, Jesus states, 'Your word is truth' (v.17). There is no reservation and no exclusion. The Word of God is truth. On no subject did Jesus place the Scripture under criticism.

Of the prophets we read: 'God ... spoke in time

past to the fathers by the prophets' (Heb. 1:1). They professed to be proclaiming what God said. Nowhere in the whole of the Old Testament is there any hint that what they wrote is anything other than the truth of God's Word. 'Forever, O LORD, Your word is settled in heaven' (Ps. 119:89). The Word is unchangeable, eternal and true.

Paul says: 'All Scripture is given by inspiration of God' (2 Tim. 3:16). If it is divinely inspired, men ought to receive it with reverence. The writers of Scripture did not utter at random the statements we have received from them but they testified to truth by the Spirit of the Lord. That same Spirit who spoke through them testifies in our hearts to the truth of their message. If it proceeds from God, then it comes from the fountain of truth and is wholly true.

The Bible contains truth and nothing but truth. The writings of other faiths and philosophies have at times truth mixed with error, or truth mixed with the endorsement of questionable moral practices. Sometimes they have scientific aberrations and incorrect statements. But the Bible has no scientific error and no incorrect deductions. Furthermore, what moral or spiritual truth for the good of man can be found outside the Bible? It is sufficient in itself and is complete in its total moral scope. If other books were lost and the Bible retained, there would still be a huge volume of moral and spiritual teaching. But if the Bible were lost and all the other books retained there would be an irreparable loss.

The Bible is sufficient as a moral and spiritual guide.

It reveals God as a God of love and of holiness. It reveals man as a sinner condemned by the righteousness of God but loved by the God who is love. It reveals that God in His love executed a plan by which He projected Himself into this world in the person of His Son who became the Substitute for man in his sin and condemnation. He, Jesus, identified Himself with our sin and bore our punishment so that we could be forgiven and released from sinful bondage to live for the One who saved us. To all who trust Him, He is found to be an abundant Saviour. The deepest needs in the heart of man are met.

In whatever nation or culture, and under whatever teaching or philosophy, sin is wrong, and evil is hurtful and destructive. Envy, jealousy, pride, impurity, hatred and a host of other evils surge within humanity, and pain and hurt are the result. There are broken hearts, broken lives and broken homes everywhere. Sin has destroyed beautiful relationships, has damaged lives irreparably and has left its trail of sorrow everywhere. Man has a conscience which records such hurt, and a life which feels the cuts and bruises, the pain and grief of wrong in its numerous forms. That open wound must be healed, that hurt must be relieved, that breach repaired, the pain removed, the enmity reconciled, the sin forgiven, the attitudes righted, the damaged soul retrieved and repaired. These are the common needs of all men.

What book can tell us how to rid ourselves of the intolerable burden of sin and wrong but the Bible? What book can offer peace from a troubled conscience, peace from the burden of guilt and sin, but the Bible? There is no other book which can offer salvation from the heavy burden and cruel grief of sin. Buddhism with its meditation and ethics, Confucianism with its philosophies and idealism, Hinduism with its synchronised religion and its extreme idolatry, Shintoism with its variety and mythology, Islam with its rigidity, its distant god, its lack of provision for sin – they all fail to bring the relief and joy of forgiveness, and the peace of a soul rightly related to God. The deepest need of man remains unfulfilled and the hurt and sin live on to sear and damage the whole personality. Sin has not been removed and there is no forgiveness to bring relief, peace and joy to man's seeking heart.

Only the Bible has the answer. 'You shall call His name JESUS, for He will save His people from their sins' (Matt. 1:21). God has a plan, a method, whereby I can be rid of my sin for ever! Jesus, my Saviour, has taken my sin upon Himself and has taken my punishment so that I can be free from sin's oppressive load, from sin's enslaving power, from sin's defilement. I can be healed. The relief and joy of salvation are mine in Jesus. He is the way back to God.

Here lies the truth about my relationship with God. The truth is in Jesus. 'Therefore if the Son makes you free, you shall be free indeed' (John

8:36). Here is liberty; here is salvation; here is emancipation; here is healing! It is in Jesus, the way, the truth and the life. Jesus Himself said, 'no man comes to the Father, but by me'. He is the only way and the Bible is the only book that shows the way of salvation and meets the needs of man. Trust the One who died to save you, who lives to pray for you, who is coming to receive you – if you know Him – for all eternity!

Chapter 7

ITS ABILITY

The symbols of the Bible indicate its realm of activity and its power and authority. The Bible has remarkable insight into the soul of man, and is able to analyse the condition of the human heart with unerring accuracy and expose the flaws with conclusive truthfulness. Its symbols show us its activity.

The Symbols of the Bible

1. *It is like a Sword.* 'Take ... the sword of the Spirit, which is the Word of God' (Eph. 6:17). 'For the word of God is sharper than any two-edged sword' (Heb. 4:12).

It cuts to the quick and pierces the heart. Its sharp pointed statements penetrate the soul's strongest armour and lay bare the thoughts and intentions of the heart. It slices away surface cover and reveals the cancers of the soul.

2. *It is like a Fire.* 'Is not My word like a fire?' (Jer. 23:29).

Fire illuminates the dark and sinister places, it melts the hardest of hearts, it consumes and burns up sin, it purifies from evil, it destroys all that is contrary to God's holy requirements.

127

Yet fire melts and welds together the hearts of God's children. Fire attracts and gives warmth as they study its truths. Fire spreads from one heart to another. Ah, the wonderful Word of God! What other book can make hearts glow and burn as believers pour over its truths?

3. *It is like a Hammer* 'that breaks the rock in pieces' (Jer. 23:29).

The hardest heart may resist the sword and the fire, but the hammer smashes and demolishes evil. It shatters the devious carnal schemes and intrigues, it destroys the iniquitous rebellion of man. Under the hammer of God's Word, sin's power is broken and the soul is released from its clutches.

4. *It is like a Mirror* (James 1:23-25)

God says that if someone hears the Word but does nothing about it, he is like a person who looks in a mirror and forgets what he sees. The mirror shows us what is there, and enables us to right any defects. The mirror exposes, it reveals, it exhibits, it unmasks, it discloses, it lays bare the condition of the heart. It is a diagnostic tool, making us aware of a condition which needs attention, and then leading us to Christ who alone is able to deal with our sin and our problems. As we read God's Word we see ourselves as needy souls before Him. Uncannily it exposes our condition. While we are reading the Bible, the Bible is reading us. The Bible is the mirror of the soul. No other book has this effect.

5. *It is like a Lamp.* 'Your word is a lamp to my feet and a light to my path' (Ps. 119:105).

The Bible has been given to guide us. A light on the path shows the way ahead, a lamp shows the next step. The Bible lights the sinner's path to Christ and the believer's path to heaven. How can a book written so long ago give advice on contemporary issues? Only because its message is given by the One who created us all and knows our human needs. It is a book for every age, for it comes from the ageless One, and its message is timeless.

6. *It is like Seed.* 'Been born again, not of corruptible seed but incorruptible, through the word of God which lives and abides for ever' (I Pet. 1:23).

The Seed is planted in men's hearts and there it germinates. It is a life-producing, life-imparting Word. New life brings with it new desires and an entirely new lifestyle. The old ways are discarded and new life finds expression in the joyful service of God. There are new values and new standards. Sin is avoided, righteousness is embraced; and this all because the Seed has planted new life in man's mind and heart. Man is indeed a new creation. What other book can do that?

7. *It is like Water.* 'That He might sanctify and cleanse it with the washing of water by the word' (Eph. 5:26).

Water is a cleansing agent. Jesus said, 'You are already clean because of the word which I have spoken to you' (John 15:3). As believing men and

129

women soak in the Word, the Word becomes life to them and its principles of purity and righteousness permeate their lives. They want to do what God wants them to do, and as God is holy, so their lives become holy. The word cleanses. Can any other book claim to constantly cleanse the life?

Water is refreshing and life-giving; so too is the Word of God.

8. *It is like Milk*. '... desire the pure milk of the word' (I Pet. 2:2).

The Word is rich spiritual sustenance which nourishes those who have put their trust in God. It is a provision for health and growth, and those who drink of its satisfying stream find it laden with an abundance of inexhaustible sufficiency. It satisfies the needs of the human heart. Shakespeare, Dickens and other literary giants thrill the aesthetic tastes but here is a volume which goes deeper than them all. It feeds not only the mind but the soul as well.

9. *It is like Meat*. 'But solid food belongs to those who are of full age' (Heb. 5:14).

Milk feeds the young but meat the full grown. The Bible meets the needs of the inexperienced in spiritual things as well as those who are already grounded in the principles of the faith. No group is excluded. It satisfies everyone's needs, enabling the simple to rejoice in its salvation and the learned to grapple with and thrill at the deep revelations within that salvation. God's Word meets everyone at the level of their understanding and at the point of their need.

130

10. *It is like Bread.* 'Man shall not live by bread alone, but by every word that proceeds from the mouth of God' (Matt 4:4).

To those who have found new life in Christ, this insignificant book which they had formerly discarded as irrelevant and remote, incredibly becomes all-absorbing and marvellously satisfying. It is food for the hungry soul. They feed upon its teachings and find such uplift and strength from its promises, exhortations, encouragement and challenges. It is ever fresh and ready for daily consumption. To the youngest Christian and to the oldest saint, the Word is sustenance and strength.

11. *It is like Honey.* '... sweeter also than honey and the honeycomb' (Ps. 19:10).

The more it is read, pondered, memorized and studied, the more it is loved. Other books give delight and enjoyment but this Book gives far more. The marvellous phrases which clothe wonderful eternal truths never cease to thrill, fascinate and instil awe and wonder, as the delicacy and precision, purity and preciousness of these eternal truths are grasped and held. The Word is sweeter than honey. The prophet Jeremiah exclaimed that he found God's Word and ate it, 'and Your word was to me the joy and rejoicing of my heart' (Jer. 15:16).

12. *It is like Gold.* 'The judgments of the Lord ... more to be desired are they than gold' (Ps. 19:9 and 10).

Those who study the Word are enriched beyond

measure. The Bible is of priceless value. It is an inexhaustible gold mine where one can dig out treasures for ever. Some of the greatest minds in the world have spent their lives delving into this mine and have confessed that they have only scratched the surface. No other book is so profound, so fertile, so saturated with abounding riches.

13. *It is like an Anchor* '... This hope we have as an anchor of the soul' (Heb. 6:17-19).

After the storms at sea, the ship drops anchor in the harbour — safe and sound. There is security, certainty, assurance, joy and gladness in the sure knowledge that we are in Christ for all eternity. God will not break His word. We have confidence in His integrity and promises. He has promised that if we trust savingly in Christ alone for salvation, we will be with Him for ever. This is our anchor and certainty. Who would not trust such a God who gives such a promise? We trust and rejoice.

A study of the symbols shows clearly the immense power of the Word of God. It is eternal (I Pet. 1:25); it is pure (Prov. 30:5); it is trustworthy (Luke 21:33); it is alive and it is powerful (Heb. 4:12.)

The Power of the Bible
John Calvin, in his *Institutes*, describes how the Bible affects people:

'Now this power which is peculiar to Scripture is clear from the fact that of human writings, however artfully

132

polished, there is none capable of affecting us all comparably. Read Demosthenes or Cicero; read Plato, Aristotle, and others of that tribe. They will, I admit, allure you, delight you, move you, enrapture you in wonderful measure. But betake yourself from them to this sacred reading. Then, in spite of yourself, so deeply will it affect you, so penetrate your heart, so fix itself in your very marrow, that compared with its deep impression, such vigour as the orators and philosophers have will nearly vanish. Consequently, it is easy to see that the Sacred Scriptures, which so far surpasses all gifts and graces of human endeavour, breathe something divine.'[1]

1. The Bible brings Conviction

Explain it as we may, the Bible possesses the strange power of opening the eyes of men to their true condition. It shows them that they are sinners before a holy God. It brings such conviction and condemnation of their sin that many who have never seen a Bible before are overwhelmed by a deep sorrow of heart at their misdeeds. They see the vileness of their nature and they are in agony at the sight; so much so that many have endured sleepless nights as they have faced up to their sin. It seems as if their lives are opened up to the searching, sifting scrutiny of the Word. Every nook and cranny is exposed to the light and every sin pursued and hunted. Evil is brought to the surface and seen in all its revolting deformity and wretchedness. It seems as if God Himself is speaking to them through the words of Scripture. They are aware of a keen, piercing, penetrating, inward examination. They are

133

cornered and cannot escape from the thrust of the Scriptures. The Word convinces them of their sin and evil.

Throughout the history of Israel, the Word has played a major part in turning people from their sin and restoring them to grace. The great revival under Josiah was brought about by the discovery of the Word of God. Hilkiah the priest found the book of the law which had been forgotten in the temple. The book was read before the king, and 'when the king heard the words of the Law ... he tore his clothes. Then the king commanded ... Go, inquire of the LORD for me, concerning the words of the book that is found; for great is the wrath of the LORD that is poured out on us, because our fathers have not kept the word of the LORD, to do according to all that is written in this book' (2 Chron. 34:14-21).

In the days before the captivity, Baruch read the prophecy of Jeremiah in the house of the Lord. When he later read it before the princes, 'they looked in fear ... and said to Baruch, "We will surely tell the king of all these words".' The scroll was brought and read before king Jehoiakim, who 'cut it with the scribe's knife and cast it into the fire that was on the hearth, until all the roll was consumed'. Jeremiah wrote another roll and added words to the original. God had pronounced a terrible judgment upon them and it soon came to pass (Jer. 36). The word was rejected and the judgment fell.

The great and wonderful revival under Ezra and Nehemiah after the Babylonian captivity came about by the public reading of Scripture. Ezra 'stood on a platform of wood ... and opened the book in the sight of all the people ... and all the people wept, when they heard the words of the Law' (Neh. 8:1-9).

When Peter preached his great sermon at Pentecost, he quoted liberally from the Old Testament, both from the prophets and the psalms. The people were deeply convicted and cried out, 'Men and brethren, what shall we do?' The preaching of the Word brought a dreadful awareness of sin. Paul declares, 'the law entered, that the offense might abound' (Rom. 5:20). The object of the reading, of the proclamation, was the realization of sin. Guilt assumed alarming proportions and only then would they acknowledge their sinful condition and flee to God for mercy.

When the Word flies like an arrow to the heart, people become so aware of their lost condition that they cry out with the woman of Samaria, 'He told me all that I ever did' (John 4:39).

All over the world where the Word is preached, it has the same effect, bringing men under conviction of sin, and then, as they trust its promises, it releases them to all that God so lavishly gives in Christ Jesus.

In Stornoway, Isle of Lewis, Scotland, a team of Christian workers was holding an open-air campaign in the town square. It was a quiet evening and the speaker's voice echoed down Cromwell Street. Two young men crossed the street and laughed in derision as they heard the words, 'O turn

ye, O turn ye, for why will ye die, O house of Israel.'
They climbed the steps of the town hall in
anticipation of an evening of pleasure, when the
words came ringing down the street once again, 'O
turn ye, O turn ye, for why will ye die, O house of
Israel.' Suddenly one of those young men was
gripped by a tremendous sense of conviction of sin.
He stood as the Word of God burnt its way into his
heart. Leaving his companion on the steps, he ran
all the way home, a distance of about a mile, flung
himself on his knees at the side of his bed and sought
God desperately for salvation. That young man
came to Christ that day and subsequently served
God as a missionary in Africa for years. The Word
of God was as an arrow to his heart. It pierced his
armour, found its mark and accomplished its
purpose, bringing not only conviction but
conversion as well.

2. The Bible brings Regeneration

'Been born again ... through the word of God' (1
Pet. 1:23). 'By which have been given to us
exceedingly great and precious promises, that
through these you may be partakers of the divine
nature....' (2 Pet. 1:4).

Regeneration, or being born again, is an act of
God by which divine life is implanted in man. Deity
indwells humanity; God indwells man; 'Christ in
you, the hope of glory!' (Col. 1:27).

Paul tells us that it is the Spirit of God who
causes us to know the things that God freely gives

us (1 Cor. 2:12). We read that it was God who opened the heart of Lydia the seller of purple (Acts 16:14). It is therefore God who takes His Word, applies it to hearts and brings about the mighty transformation. His words have been written down by men, and His Spirit now takes His written word and speaks it to the heart. It has life-giving power. As Jesus commanded Lazarus to come out of the tomb, so the Word of God is living and powerful and has the same effect upon those who are dead in their sins when the Spirit of God speaks the Word to them.

We are made 'new creatures' in Christ (2 Cor. 5:17). We have new delights, new desires, new aspirations, new goals. We are transformed by the life of God within us. We cannot but be different! We have become a 'new man', having put off the old man with his deeds, and being renewed in the knowledge of Christ (Col. 3:10). He has placed our feet on a new and living way (Heb. 10:20).

The two great illustrations from history are Augustine and Luther. Augustine had a very chequered existence, entering into all kinds of sin and false teaching. His godly mother, Monica, prayed for him constantly. In Milan, Italy, he heard Ambrose preach and was drawn to God. Two friends counselled him, but he was still confused and in a wretched state of mind and soul. One day in the garden, he heard children chanting nearby, 'Take and read! Take and read!' He went indoors, opened the Bible, and his eye fell on Romans 13:14,

'But put ye on the Lord Jesus Christ, and make not provision for the flesh, to fulfil the lusts thereof.' He read no further. In an instant he trusted Christ for salvation, and the darkness of all his doubts vanished as God's light poured into his soul. He became one of the greatest theologians the church has ever produced.

Martin Luther tried desperately to please God. His restless, questing soul found no peace. He lectured on Galatians, Psalms and then on Romans. One day that marvellous text 'the just shall live by faith' (Rom. 1:17) found its mark, and Luther saw that all his efforts, his mortification, his sincerity, availed him nothing. He believed and trusted in God for salvation through Christ by faith alone. Thus was born the great reformer of Germany. The Word was enough. His life was transformed, the Reformation took root all over Europe, proclaiming that salvation was by Christ alone, by grace alone, by blood alone, by faith alone!

All over the world men's lives have been transformed from sin and selfishness to lives of joy and holiness through the Word. I stood on the steps of a church after a Sunday morning service enjoying the sight of about 150 Christians standing around talking and rejoicing in their salvation. An elderly member tapped me on the arm, and said, 'You see all those people – not one over four years of age.' God had worked mightily in a short time and many had trusted Christ for salvation. They had been not only respectable people, but drunkards, gamblers and drug addicts as well, and they came from all walks of life. Now they were transformed by the mighty power of God. His Word had entered their hearts and they had responded to the love of God in Christ. They had received Him and had been born from above by the Spirit of the living God.

It happens all over. I have sat around the black pot in African huts with people with whom I have had little in common save the gospel of God's grace. Dipping my hand into the pot which stood over the smouldering embers, I drew out the food and ate together with them all. Very primitive surroundings perhaps, but oh, the fellowship in the Lord – how sweet, how precious. Why, but a few years ago they were living in heathen darkness with every kind of superstition and evil practice, and now here they were rejoicing together in the salvation of God. They were new creatures in Christ Jesus! What made the change? The Word of God was read, preached, taught and applied. They heard, they were convicted of their sin, they repented and confessed their sin, they cried for mercy and laid hold on the promises of God. God Almighty came from heaven itself and entered their lives. They were born of the Spirit; they were born again. They became children of God!

Bible Societies all over the world publish magazines in which thousands of stories are told of the power of the Word of God. People come across the Bible or portions of Scripture in a variety of ways, some quite extraordinary, and as they read the Word of God, they are convinced of its truth, and transformed by its power. They, in turn, read it to others who believe and are changed.

Bibles have been distributed in prisons resulting in many coming to faith in Christ. Dangerous, evil men have been changed completely and emerge from prison to be useful members of the community and a benefit to society. Numerous reports tell of changed lives in prisons all over the world. The Bible can change the very nature of hardened criminals.

Groups and villages sometimes have been converted simply by obtaining a portion of the Word of God. In India, for instance, a man bought a packet of Scripture portions and returned to his village. A few months later when a Christian worker was asked to go to the village and speak to those who had become Christians simply by reading these books, he found that forty people had come to believe in Jesus. This is no isolated instance. Many such stories are to be found in Bible Society publications.

Here is another report concerning a drunkard in East Nepal who bought a Gospel portion. 'He read and reread the book with deep interest. As he read, he found he began to believe. He believed on the Lord Jesus Christ as his Saviour and Lord, and found his whole life changed. He told his family and they believed; he told his friends in the village and they too believed. He had never seen a Bible or even heard of Jesus Christ until he read that Gospel portion.'

The Word of God has tremendous power. Simple people, educated people, young people, old people, poor people – all recognize the innate authority, convicting truth and transforming power of God's living Word. They yield to its authority and trust in Jesus as Saviour and Lord, experiencing the wonderful peace of His forgiveness and the joy of new life in Christ.

The Word of God has regenerating power! In millions of cases the Word has reached those in deepest degradation and has lifted them up, up, up! The Book changes individuals, alters communities, transforms nations. It cleanses the besmirched and defiled; it purifies the contaminated and degenerate; it heals the spiritually diseased; it strengthens the languishing soul; it ennobles the flagging spirit. The Word of God has mighty power.

3. *The Bible produces Faith*

Without faith it is impossible to please God (Heb. 11:6), so faith must be exercised – but in what, or in whom? The Bible tells us and inspires faith. 'Faith comes by hearing, and hearing by the word of God' (Rom. 10:17).

The Bible teems with promises. It has been estimated that there are 7,000 promises in the Bible. It is certainly difficult to count or estimate these, but however many promises there may be, the promises are sure. God cannot lie and the Scriptures cannot be broken.

Jesus says, '... he who believes in Me, though

he may die, he shall live' (John 11:25). The Bible says, 'As many as received Him, to them He gave the right to become children of God' (John 1:12). Again we read, 'He who has the Son has life' (1 John 5:12). If we believe, that is to trust in, rely on, cling to and depend upon these words spoken by God Himself, He will make them true in us. Faith in God, who speaks the words to us, is brought about by the Holy Spirit who applies the Word and creates faith in the mighty God who makes the promises. The promises are shafts of light in the darkness.

God promises us eternal life (John 3:16, 5:24), and it is for us to stretch out the hand of faith and take what God gives. That is faith in action. If someone holds out a pen and says, 'I give you this pen', it is not mine until I take it from him. I must believe what he says and then take from his hand that which he offers. When I do so it is mine and I find his word to be true. He has actually given me the pen. I rejoice in the gift and am grateful. Faith in his word has brought enrichment to my life. I believed, I took, I possessed.

So God gives us eternal life in Christ. He offers it to us and tells us all about it in the Bible. It is for us to realize that He means what He says and is able and willing to make good His every word. As we trust Him and receive His proffered gift, the transformation takes place in us. We receive life and we are saved by grace through faith (Eph. 2:8 and 9).

The wonderful news is that all over the world,

in large cities, in rural villages, in palaces, in humble homes, saving faith has been exercised, and men, women, boys and girls have believed the promises and received new life in Christ. Millions upon millions have been mightily transformed and rejoice in the fact that Jesus lives within them. They know Him and they love Him with all their hearts. What other book can create such miracles? What other book has had such a fantastic effect upon all those who give allegiance to its teachings and exercise faith in its promises? Lives have been altered for all eternity. Broken homes have been healed, shattered lives have been restored, love and kindness have replaced hatred and bitterness. The miracles of saving grace abound on every hand and in every land.

4. *The Bible promotes the growth of holy and righteous living*

The wonderful words of the psalmist 3000 years ago ring true today: 'How can a young man cleanse his way? By taking heed according to Your word. Your word I have hidden in my heart, that I might not sin against You' (Ps. 119:9, 11).

As we read the Bible methodically, study it faithfully, ponder it prayerfully, meditate upon it constantly, memorize it frequently and obey it instantly, we shall find that the principles of inward holiness and outward righteousness will increasingly become part of our lives.

Sinful habits fall away, and even those people

who have high ideals of culture and ethics, find that the Bible points them to a life of inward holiness and communion with God that dwarfs every human achievement and enriches them with a quality of life never known before.

The Bible is milk for the young in Christ, meat for the strong, and the finest of wheat and honey out of the rock for those who live in its truths. As people study the Bible daily and systematically, they will advance healthily, continuously and steadily from initially receiving salvation or from retarded spiritual living, to full Christian maturity.

Neglecting the Bible is like neglecting food, and this will, of course, result in hunger and stunted growth. But prayerful, daily study of the Word will result in growth in grace and in the knowledge of God. To faith is added virtue, knowledge, self-control, patience, brotherly kindness, love. As these qualities increase and abound, we grow more like the perfect Lord Jesus and find joyful fulfilment in the knowledge of God.

Jesus prayed, 'Sanctify them by Your truth. Your word is truth' (John 17:17). The Word does its own sanctifying and cleansing work as we read and study its precious truths.

Chapter 8

ITS MESSAGE

It would be pointless to have a book of such worth and value and not have it say something! It has a message – a message about God, man and salvation.

The Bible portrays God as a living and personal spiritual being with a distinct character and nature. He is not an abstract impersonal power or influence, but a person who creates and sustains all things. The Bible asserts the unity of God, 'The LORD our God, the LORD is one' (Deut. 6:4), but the nature of that unity does not exclude the idea of a plurality of persons in the Godhead. There is the Trinity of the Father, the Son and the Holy Spirit, all modes of being or persons within the Godhead. The Athanasian creed states, 'neither confounding the persons, nor dividing the substance of the Godhead.' 'There are three Centres of expression in one identical nature,' says T. C. Hammond.

This great and living God has attributes. There is the infinity of God, the self-existence of God, the eternity and immutability of God, the omniscience, omnipotence and omnipresence of God. God has moral attributes as well. There is the righteousness and justice of God, the mercy and lovingkindness of God, the holiness and love of God.

'**God is love**' (1 John 4:8) is the best known biblical definition of God. Love is the expression of His being. In His love He wants to reveal Himself and have fellowship with man. His love is everlasting (Jer. 31:3), it is universal (John 3:16), it is individual (Gal. 2:20), it is sacrificial (1 John 3:16), it is saving (Rev. 1:5). In His love He would sweep us into His tender embrace, but there is a problem, and the problem lies with us.

Man has sinned: 'For all have sinned and fall short of the glory of God' (Rom. 3:23). Everyone has sinned, and God's eternal decree stands firm, 'the soul who sins shall die' (Ezek. 18:4). In His love He would draw near, but in His holiness He must condemn. If He did not follow through with His righteous judgment and punish man with death for his sin, He would compromise His decree and negate His own holy character. But God does not lie, and the sinner must be punished. There is no escape; the whole world is held accountable to God, and judgment must be executed, 'these shall be punished with everlasting destruction' (2 Thess. 1:9); 'the wages of sin is death' (Rom. 6:23). Because all men are sinners they are doomed to die. All men must be judged, a judgment from which there is no escape. '... as it is appointed for men to die once, but after this the judgment' (Heb. 9:27). 'It is a fearful thing to fall into the hands of the living God' (Heb. 10:31).

From this fearful plight **man must find salvation**. Where can it be found? If I lived a righteous life, would that bring salvation? Man cannot save himself by his works of righteousness. Paul, speaking of salvation says, 'Not by works of righteousness which we have done, but according to His mercy He saved us' (Titus 3:5). Speaking to the Ephesians he says, 'For by grace you have been saved through faith, and that not of yourselves; it is the gift of God, not of works, lest anyone should boast' (Eph. 2:8, 9). We do not deserve salvation, because we are sinners. We cannot earn salvation, for God in His mercy gives it freely to us. '... the gift of God is eternal life in Christ Jesus our Lord' (Rom. 6:23). We cannot save ourselves by our religion. No church can save. Paul was a very religious man but his righteous, religious life did not save him. Many are trusting in church membership for salvation, but this cannot save them.

Man has a problem which neither righteousness nor religion can cure. Man has a problem with sin. It is a defilement and disease of the soul which must be cleansed and cured. Merely adding righteous deeds and religious activities to a sinful soul does not remove the sin. Something must be done to take away the sin which merits judgment. If the sin is removed, the punishment for the sin is no longer necessary and the soul can be saved. How can I get rid of my sin?

God has an infinitely wonderful plan for man's salvation. He brings His love and His justice together in the person of Jesus Christ. 'In the beginning was the Word, and the Word was with God, and the Word was God.' 'And the Word became flesh and dwelt among us ...' (John 1:1, 14). God projected Himself into the human race in the person of His Son. He was incarnated in the human Jesus, and He knew no sin and did no sin. Jesus was God in the flesh, '... who is over all, the eternally blessed God' (Rom. 9:5). 'For unto us a Child is born, unto us a Son is given ... and His name will be called Wonderful, Counsellor, Mighty God, Everlasting Father, Prince of Peace' (Is. 9:6).

In His infinite love, **God provided a Substitute, even Jesus Christ**, who, although He was sinless, identified Himself with man's sin, took it upon Himself, and as a consequence bore the punishment for that sin. 'For He made Him who knew no sin to be sin for us' (2 Cor. 5:21). 'Who Himself bore our sins in His own body on the tree' (1 Peter 2:24). '... while we were still sinners, Christ died for us' (Rom. 5:8). 'All we like sheep have gone astray; we have turned, every one, to his own way; and the LORD has laid on Him the iniquity of us all' (Is. 53:6). God hates sin and His punishment for sin falls on Jesus Christ who died in our place. Justice is meted out. God who said that the one who sins will die, has Himself in His love, provided the Substitute who dies in our place. God's holy character is untarnished. He did not lie. The just punishment has fallen. His love and grace are magnified in that sinful man is not the recipient of His wrath, but Jesus Christ is the One who bears the sin and its punishment in our place. Salvation has been accomplished and God is the author and executor of it all. Salvation is of God. He has, in this wonderful way, dealt with sin.

How is that which Jesus did 2000 years ago transferred to me? **We are saved by faith**. Faith is not merely head knowledge. Many say that they believe in God but their faith does not save them. It is an acknowledgement of a Supreme Being rather than a trust in a divine Saviour. 'You believe that there is one God. You do well. Even the demons believe – and tremble' (James 2:19). Belief is much more than an intellectual comprehension, it is a moral appropriation. It is trusting what we know to be true; and claiming the vast benefits of that knowledge personally.

Realizing that we are condemned, and realizing that we cannot save ourselves, we turn to God and ask Him to forgive us and to take away our sins for Christ our Substitute's sake. **Faith is trusting Jesus Christ alone for salvation**. 'For I am not ashamed of the gospel of Christ, for it is the power of God to salvation for everyone who believes' (Rom. 1:16). Faith is believing that God's salvation works for me now. It is taking God at His word. It is believing that when He says that He will forgive for Christ's sake, He will do just that for me – even me – now as I trust Him. 'If we confess our sins, He is faithful and just to forgive us our sins, and to cleanse us from all unrighteousness' (1 John 1:9). It is a trusting in, a resting on, a relying upon God's word as I believe what Christ has done to be true and claim it to be effective in me this very moment. A fearful jailer once asked, 'what must I do to be saved?' and he received the reply, 'Believe on the Lord Jesus Christ, and you will be saved' (Acts 16:31). That is a divine guarantee. God has promised and His promise will stand, His word will not be broken. Salvation will be experienced – you will be saved.

There are implications, the most important of which is *repentance*. God 'commandeth all men every where to repent' (Acts 17:30). He requires that we have 'repentance toward God and faith toward our Lord Jesus Christ' (Acts 20:21). 'The Lord is not slack concerning His promise, as some count slackness, but is long-suffering toward us, not willing that any should perish but that all should come to repentance' (2 Peter 3:9). Repentance means changing direction, being sorry enough to quit. We are going down the broad road leading to destruction and we turn from it to the narrow road which leads to life. It is a complete U-turn. We were serving our own selfish ends, and perhaps unknowingly, were in the service of the devil. This natural selfish life now comes to an end. We turn from our sins and our idols to serve the living and true God. 'He who covers his sins will not prosper: but whoever confesses and forsakes them will have mercy' (Prov. 28:13).

We are now under new management. We have met the Lord Jesus Christ who said, 'If anyone loves

Me, he will keep My word' (John 14:23). Our lives are now to be lived by giving attention to the wonderful instructions in His holy Word. That becomes our guide and compass. Here we find direction and purpose for life.

Not only does He forgive our sins but **He gives us His life**. Eternal life is a gift from God. 'For God so loved the world that He gave His only begotten Son' (John 3:16). 'But as many as received Him, to them He gave the right to become children of God, even to those who believe in His name' (John 1:12). 'He who has the Son has life' (1 John 5:12).

Faith then extends both negatively and positively. He says that He will forgive my sins for Christ's sake. I trust the statement and my sins are forgiven. He says that He will come into the lives of those who receive the gift of His Son. I trust the statement and receive Jesus Christ into my heart and life. As I believe, my sins are taken away (negatively) and Jesus Christ comes into my life (positively). 'By which have been given to us exceedingly great and precious promises, that through these you may be partakers of the divine nature' (2 Peter 1:4). We become partakers of God's life, and are born of His Spirit. We have the Son within us and we have new life in Christ. We are born again. We are saved. We are His children. We can now 'know that you have eternal life' (1 John 5:13). **He brings an assurance** to our hearts by His own presence and Spirit within us.

Blessed assurance, Jesus is mine,
Oh what a foretaste of glory divine.
Heir of salvation, purchase of God,
Born of His Spirit, washed in His blood.

How does the actual transaction take place? How am I saved? How do I become a child of God?

Read the following verses from the Bible: Isaiah 53:6; 1 John 1:9; John 1:12; 1 John 5:12, 13.

Bow in prayer and proceed step by step.

'Oh God I confess that I am a sinner.

I cannot save myself. My good works are not sufficient.

I am sorry for my sins and shortcomings.

I ask Your forgiveness for all my sins. Please forgive me for Christ's sake as I sincerely repent of all my sins.

I believe that Jesus is the Son of God who died for me on the cross. He is the only one who can forgive me and make me a child of God.

Lord Jesus come into my life, to be my personal Saviour and Lord. Come in as I trust You. I receive you now.

I believe that you have heard my prayer. Your promises stand. You have forgiven me and have come into my heart. You have made me your child.

Thank you for what you have done.

In Jesus Name, Amen.

You may feel different, you may feel relieved, and then again you may have no feelings whatever. Feelings are not the ground of salvation. The Word of God is the foundation of it all. God has said that He will forgive and come into the life of the one who repents and trusts in Him. That is the basis of my faith and salvation. I trust what He has said whether I feel anything or nothing. As I continue to trust, the witness of the Spirit in my heart or the assurance which God Himself brings by His inward presence, will come, and I will know most certainly that I have been born of God. God communicates that knowledge to us by His Spirit within. It is an inward understanding, a glad realization that I am His.

May God grant that many will come to trust this wonderful Saviour and find in Him an all-sufficient, glorious Lord and loving Friend to the end of life's journey.

This is not the end. This is the beginning. Have a daily time of prayer. Read the Bible methodically, prayerfully, daily. Obey what God says to you in His word. Obedience is essential for joy, growth and usefulness in the Christian life. Should you fail and sin, go immediately to Him and ask His forgiveness. Tell others what God has done for you. This confirms your faith and you are now being used to spread God's wonderful news of salvation. Meet with others in a Bible-believing church or fellowship where you will be encouraged and taught. Serve the Lord with gladness.

REFERENCES

Chapter 1 – Its Unity

1. Torrey, R. A., *The Bible and its Christ*, Fleming H. Revel, New York, 1904, p.26.
2. Pache, Rene, *The Inspiration and Authority of Scripture*, Moody, Chicago, 1969, p.113.
3. Scroggie, W. G., *The Unfolding Drama of Redemption*, Vol. 1. Pickering & Inglis, London, 1953, p.31.
4. Bancroft, Emery H., *Christian Theology*, Zondervan, Grand Rapids, 1976, p.49.
5. Rowley, H. H., *The Unity of the Bible*, Carey Kingsgate Press, London, 1953, p. 52.
6. Snaith, Norman H., *The Distinctive Ideas of the Old Testament*, Shochan Books, New York, 1964, pp. 46, 47.
7. ibid. pp. 59, 60.

Chapter 2 – Its Inherent Authority

1. Evans, William, *The Great Doctrine of the Bible*, Moody, Chicago, 1949, p.203.
2. Vine, W. E., *Collected Writings of W. E. Vine*, Gospel Tract, Glasgow, 1985, p.45.
3. ibid. p.37.
4. Munhall, L. W., *Inspiration in the Fundamentals*, Edited by R. A. Torrey, Kregel, Grand Rapids, 1990, p.159.
5. Milne, Bruce, *Know the Truth*, IVP, Leicester, 1982, p.31.
6. Prof. Milligan in W. G. Scroggie, *Is the Bible the Word of God?* Oliphants, n.d., p.57.
7. ibid. p.57.

8. ibid. p.50.

9. Prof. Orr, *Revelation & Inspiration*, p.190, quoted in Vine, p. 50.

10. Scroggie, W. G., *Is the Bible the Word of God?* p.54.

11. Evans, W., *The Great Doctrines of the Bible*, Moody, Chicago, 1949, p.94.

12. ibid. pp. 201-202.

13. ibid. p.209.

Chapter 3 – Its Endorsement by Christ

1. MacIntyre, David M., *The Divine Authority of the Scriptures of the Old Testament*, Drummond's Tract Depot, Stirling, London, 1902, p.66.

2. Bishop Moule in Scroggie, *Is the Bible the Word of God?*.

Chapter 4 – Its Prophecy

1. Scroggie, W. G., *Is the Bible the Word of God?*, pp. 41, 42.

2. Conner, K. J., *The Foundations of Christian Doctrine*. Sovereign World, Tonbridge, 1980, pp. 30-33.

3. Bishop Westcott in Scroggie, *Is the Bible the Word of God?*, p.39.

Chapter 5 – Its Archaeology

1. Unger, M. F., *Archaeology and the Old Testament*, Zondervan, Grand Rapids, 1954, p.16.

2. Wiseman, D. J., *Illustrations from Biblical Archaeology*, Tyndale, London, 1958, p.25.

3. ibid. p.27.

4. Thomson, J. A., *Archaeology and the Old Testament*, Eerdmans, Grand Rapids, 1957, p.17.

5. Unger, p.111.

6. Wiseman, p.27.

7. Unger, p.123.

8. Thomson, p.31.

9. Unger, p.121.

10. ibid. p.130.

11. Caiger, S. L. 1938, *The Old Testament and Moswen Discovery*, S.P.C.K., p.22.

12. Thomson, p.60.

13. Unger, p.200.

14. ibid. p.217.

15. Thomson, p.84.

16. Unger, p.227.

17. ibid. p.230.

18. Grollenberg, L. H., *Atlas of the Bible*, Thomas Nelson, London, 1956, p.74.

19. Unger, p.244.

20. ibid. p.16.

21. ibid. p.16.

22. Arnot, A. B., *Why I Believe My Bible*, Albion Press, Cape Town, 1953, p.23.

23. Thomson, p.56.

24. Caiger, p.29.

25. Unger, M. F., *Archaeology and the New Testament*, Zondervan, Grand Rapids, 1962, p.21.

26. ibid. p.22.

27. ibid. p.23.

28. ibid. p.245.

29. ibid. p.25.

30. ibid. p.195

31. ibid. p.219.

32. ibid. p.229.

33. ibid. p.57.

34. ibid. p.158.

Chapter 6 – Its Superiority

1. Hastings, James (Ed), *Dictionary of the Bible* (12th Imp.), Vol. 1. T. & T. Clark, Edinburgh, 1936, pp.293 and 294.

2. Hume, Robert E., *The World's Living Religion*, Charles Scribner's Sons, New York, 1959, p.122.

3. Hastings, p.295.

4. Boa, Kenneth, *Cults, World Religions and You*, Victor Books (SP) Wheaton, Ill, 1977, p.16.

5. ibid. p.45.

6. ibid. p.48.

7. Bouquet, A. C., *Sacred Books of the World*, Penguin Books, 1954, p.286.

8. Boa, p.55.

9. Copleston, F.S., *Christ or Mohammed?*, Nuprint, Harpenden, Herts, 1989, p.383.

10. ibid. p.390.

11. ibid. p.391.

12. ibid. p.428.

13. Henderson, George, *The Wonderful Word*, McCall Barbour, Edinburgh, n.d., p.112.

14. Lee, Robert, *The Outlined Bible*, Pickering & Inglis, n.d., London.

Chapter 7 – Its Ability

1. Calvin's *Institutes*, Volume I, p.94.

Christian Focus Publications publishes biblically-accurate books for adults and children. The books in the adult range are published in three imprints.

Christian Heritage contains classic writings from the past.

Christian Focus contains popular works including biographies, commentaries, doctrine, and Christian living.

Mentor focuses on books written at a level suitable for Bible College and seminary students, pastors, and others; the imprint includes commentaries, doctrinal studies, examination of current issues, and church history.

For a free catalogue of all our titles, please write to
Christian Focus Publications,
Geanies House, Fearn,
Ross-shire, IV20 1TW, Great Britain

For details of our titles visit us on our web site
http://www.christianfocus.com

Rev. Dr. Colin N. Peckham, LTh Hons, BA, (Theol), BTh Hons, MTh, DTh, was born in South Africa where he had ten years of evangelistic ministry and youth work before entering Bible College work in Cape Town. He is at present principal of The Faith Mission Bible College, 2 Drum Street, Gilmerton, Edinburgh, Scotland, where he is lecturing and from where he has an extensive preaching ministry in Great Britain and abroad.